SEXUALITY

JEFFREY WEEKS
Social Work Studies Department
University of Southampton

London and New York

First published in 1986 by Ellis Horwood Ltd
and Tavistock Publications Ltd

Simultaneously published in the USA and Canada
by Routledge
a division of Routledge, Chapman and Hall Inc.
29 West 35th Street, New York, NY 10001

Reprinted 1989, 1990 and 1991

Phototypeset in Times by Ellis Horwood Ltd
Printed in Great Britain by Richard Clay Ltd, Bungay, Suffolk

British Library Cataloguing in Publication Data

Sexuality.—(Key ideas)
  1. Sex
  I. Title II. Series
  306.7   HQ21

ISBN 0-415-03954-1

Contents

Jeffrey Weeks currently works in educational administration in London, and is a Visiting Fellow at the University of Southampton. He was previously a Research Fellow and lecturer at the Universities of Essex, Kent and Southampton. His extensive research and writing on sexuality since the mid 1970's has produced such important contributions to the field as *Coming Out: Homosexual Politics in Britain from the 19th Century to the Present*; *Sex, Politics and Society*; and *Sexuality and its Discontents*.

Editor's foreword

We are, as Jeffrey Weeks points out in this book, almost programmed into thinking of our sexuality as a wholly natural feature of life. It is of course a truism that sexual relations are but one form of social relations, but we are nonetheless accustomed to think also of social relations as 'natural', at least in the commonsense world. Yet it is the task of sociology and the other social sciences to 'deconstruct' naturalism, and to determine how actions are given their meaning and significance via social interaction. Why in principle should not sexuality be treated as socially conditioned phenomenon as, say, chess-playing or cuisine? The liberationist philosophies of the post-war generation have accustomed us to a search for a 'natural' and unrepressed sexuality, as if there were at bottom some essential form of sexual relations whose expression lies in an extra-moral domain. Yet simultaneously the same generation has also been the site of a resurgence of homosexuality, of transvestism, of pederasty, and of fierce and critical debate about the negotiation of gender identity. As the philosopher-historian Michel Foucault pointed out, sexuality is no more (or no less) than a historical construct. Its meaning and expression is no wider or extensive than its specific social or historical manifestations, and explaining its forms and variations cannot be accomplished without examining and explaining the context in which they are located.

Jeffrey Weeks has written extensively on what we might call the new sociology of sexuality, and is representative of the way in which what was a slightly 'marginal' academic interest has come to full respectability. It is slightly ironic that sexuality should appear to have increased its hold over aspects of popular culture (cf. the mass of sexual media currently available in Western societies and the ubiquity of sexual imagery in advertising) at the same time as the new perspectives on sexuality attempt to deconstruct it as a cultural expression. However, our preoccupation with sexuality does mean that it is more necessary than ever to interpret and elucidate this all-pervasive ideology.

One important feature of the present interest in sexuality is its linkage with a parallel concern with questions of family, kinship and household organization. The massive expansion of 'family history' as a site of academic research, has itself more empiric parallels in the growth of social policy initiatives, social intervention in the lives of families, indeed the emergence of a field of bio-politics in which the state can be seen as attempting to regulate and control. Both psychological and social therapies devote great attention to the sexual dimension of their clients' lives. This is not perhaps an entirely new feature of social control — for the Church and the village community were at least as concerned about regulating and organizing sexual behaviour in Western societies of the pre-industrial era, as is the modern state. But what is different and qualitatively new is the attention paid to the rationalization of sexuality, and its subjection to scientific study, in modern Western society.

In the detailed and carefully argued discussion of the sociology of sexuality which Jeffrey Weeks has written, the connection of sexuality to its socio-historical context is explored in ways which reveal just how completely sex is socially constructed. This naturally raises problems about sexual morality which are likely to cause a certain amount of unease. For if sexuality is at base a social convention of almost infinite variety, then nothing is either 'right' or 'wrong'. Clearly — as Weeks is concerned to stress — the issue cannot be left there. We are rational and intelligent beings who have the capacity to choose the moral codes under which we live — or at least to negotiate modifications and adaptations to them.

Peter Hamilton

Acknowledgements

It is now over ten years since I first began writing on the history and sociology of sex. During that time I have incurred many intellectual and emotional debts. There is no space here to record the names of all the people who have helped me. I refer readers to the acknowledgements in my previous books, full details of which are given in 'Suggestions for further reading' at the end of this book. All I can do here is to thank them all once again, and to free them from any obligation to agree with everything (or anything) I say here.

Some debts are immediate, however. I must thank Peter Hamilton for asking me to write this book, Caradoc King for encouraging me to do so, Barbara Giddins for patiently transferring my early drafts into legible type which allowed me to rethink, rejig and rewrite, and Janet Hussein for (as ever) typing an impeccable final draft. My gratitude, as always, goes to Chetan Bhatt, Micky Burbidge and Angus Suttie for sustaining me during its writing. But my greatest debt is to my students, whose questions, doubts, anxieties and stimulation have forced me to think through many of the issues I tackle here. I therefore dedicate this book to my students — past, present and (government policy permitting) future. I hope they get as much from this essay as I got from them.

1

The languages of sex

Sex is an either/or phenomenon — appealing or appalling, rarely in between.

Murray S. Davis [1]

The more expert we become in talking about sexuality, the greater the difficulties we seem to encounter in trying to understand it. Despite sustained attempts over many years to 'demystify' sex, and several decades of much proclaimed — or condemned — 'liberalism' and 'permissiveness', the erotic still arouses acute moral anxiety and confusion. This is not because sex is intrinsically 'naughty', as a sensitive commentator has rightly remarked, but 'because it is a focus for powerful feelings' [2]. The strong emotions it undoubtedly arouses gives to the world of sexuality a seismic sensitivity making it a transmission belt for a wide variety of needs and desires: for love and anger, tenderness and agression, intimacy and adventure, romance and predatoriness, pleasure and pain, empathy and power. We experience sex very subjectively.

At the same time, the very mobility of sexuality, its chameleon-like ability to take many guises and forms, so that what for one might be a source of warmth and attraction, for another might be one of fear and hate, makes it a peculiarly sensitive conductor of cultural influences, and hence of social and political divisions. Not surprisingly, therefore, especially during the past century, sexuality has become the focus of fierce ethical and political divisions: between traditional moralists (of various religious hues, or of none) and liberals, between the high priests of sexual restraint and the advocates of sexual liberation, between the defenders of male privilege and those such as feminists who challenged it, and between the forces of moral regulation and a host of radical sexual oppositions, some of whom attack each other as much as they oppose sexual orthodoxy.

In the past such debates might have been regarded as marginal to the mainstream of political life, whatever their importance for those closely involved. Increasingly over the past decades, however, sexual issues have moved closer to the centre of political concerns. In North America and Europe the 'New Right' has recently mobilized considerable political energies through its emphasis on the so-called 'social issues': an affirmation of the sanctity of family life, hostility to homosexuality and 'sexual deviance', opposition to sex education, and the reassertion of traditional demarcations between the sexes; all have proved powerful weapons in building new political constituencies for conservative politics. This in turn is a back-handed compliment to the success of feminism and radical sexual movements in challenging many of the received norms of sexual behaviour, identities and relationships. 'Progressive opinion' may not have quite known how to react to these challenges but there is a widespread recognition that the ground rules of the debate have irreversibly shifted. So much is clear. What is less apparent is how we are to negotiate our way through the maze that apparently constitutes 'sexuality'.

In the West, at least, sexuality has been seen as having a special relationship with the nature of virtue and truth since before the triumph of Christianity. Through our sex we are expected to find ouselves and our place in the world. What was mooted in the debates of late antiquity, codified by the early Christian disquisitions on the flesh and personalized in the procedures of the Catholic confessional and Protestant witness before God, reached an apotheosis in the last century as medicine and psychology, sexology and pedagogy, took on a role, alongside the Churches, of establishing moral and social standards. By the end of the nineteenth century, as many observed, doctors had adopted some of the attributes of a new priesthood, and many of them seemed as certain of their views as the old. But the increasing politicization of sex in the past century offers new possibilities and consequent challenges: not just of moral control, and its inevitable converse, sexual deviance, but of political analysis, opposition and of change. This makes it all the more necessary that we know what we are talking about when we speak of sexuality, that we clarify the meaning (or more accurately meanings) of this complex phenomenon. We need to know what it has been and is, before we can rationally decide what it should, or could, be.

This is an easy aim to proclaim. It is a notoriously more hazardous task to carry out. All of us have so much invested in our own concept of what is the true sex that we find it difficult enough to understand dispassionately the sexual needs and behaviour of our closest contemporaries, let alone the infinitely more ambiguous desires of our predecessors. The mists of time and the various disguises of prejudice conveniently obscure other ways of living a sexual life. This resilient will-not-to-know is backed up by an assumption which is deeply embedded in our culture: that our sexuality is the most spontaneously natural thing about us. It is the basis for some of our most passionate feelings and commitments. Through it, we experience ourselves as real people; it gives us our identities, our sense of self, as men and women, as heterosexual and homosexual, 'normal' or 'abnormal', 'natural' or 'unnatural'. Sex has become, as the French philosopher Michel Foucault famously put it, 'the truth of our being' [3]. But what is this 'truth'? And on what basis can we call something 'natural' or 'unnatural'? Who has the right to lay down the laws of sex? Sex may be 'spontaneous' and 'natural'. But it has not stopped an endless barrage of advice on how best to do it.

Let us start with the term 'sex' and its common uses. Its very ambiguity signals the difficulty. We learn very early on from many sources that 'natural' sex is what takes place with members of the 'opposite sex'. 'Sex' between people of the 'same sex' is therefore, by definition, 'unnatural'. So much is taken for granted. But the multiple meanings of the word 'sex' in these last few sentences should alert us to the real complexity of the question. The term refers both to an act and to a category of person, to a practice and to a gender. Modern culture has assumed an intimate connection between the fact of being biologically male or female (that is, having appropriate sex organs and reproductive potentialities) and the correct form of erotic behaviour (usually genital intercourse between men and women). The earliest usage of the term 'sex', in the sixteenth century, referred precisely to the division of humanity into the male section and the female section (that is, to differences of gender). The dominant meaning today, however, and one current since the early nineteenth century, refers to physical relations between the sexes, 'to have sex'. The extension of the meanings of these words indicates a shift in the way that 'sexuality' (the abstract noun referring to the quality of being 'sexual') is understood in our culture [4].

The social processes through which this has taken place are complex. But the implications are clear, for they are ones we still live with. In the first place, there is an assumption of a sharp distinction between 'the sexes', a dichotomy of interests, even an antagonism ('the battle of the sexes') which can only be precariously bridged. Men are men and women women — and rarely the twain shall meet. But secondly, there is a belief that 'sex' is an overpowering natural force, a 'biological imperative' mysteriously located in the genitals (especially the wayward male organs) that sweeps all before it (at least if you are male) like hamlets before an avalanche and that somehow bridges this divide, like a rainbow over a chasm. Thirdly, this gives rise to a pyramidical model of sex, to a sexual hierarchy stretching downwards from the apparently Nature-endowed correctness of heterosexual genital intercourse to the bizarre manifestations of 'the perverse' hopefully safely buried at the base but unfortunately always erupting in dubious places.

This view of the world of sex is deeply embedded in our culture, part of the air we breathe. It provides an ideological justification for uncontrollable male lust, and even, therefore, for the fact of rape, for the downgrading of female sexual autonomy, and for the way we treat those sexual minorities who are different from ourselves, as well as for the more acceptable verities of love, relationships and security. Since the late nineteenth century, moreover, this approach has had the ostensibly scientific endorsement of the broad tradition known as sexology, the 'science of desire'. Sexologists such as Krafft-Ebing, Havelock Ellis, August Forel, Magnus Hirschfeld, Sigmund Freud and many others, sought to discover the true meaning of sex by exploring its various guises: the experience of infantile sexuality, relations between the sexes, the influence of the 'germ plasm', the hormones and chromosomes, the nature of the 'sexual instinct', and the causes of sexual perversions. They often disagreed with one another; they frequently contradicted themselves. In the end, even the most dedicated had to admit to a certain defeat. Freud confessed to the difficulty of agreeing 'any generally recognized criterion of the sexual nature of a process' [5], and although today we may claim to be a little more confident in knowing what is 'sexual' or not, we are still in as much of a fog as those pioneers in interpreting its implications.

Sexology has had important positive effects in extending our knowledge of sexual behaviours and I have no desire to denigrate its real achievements. Without it we would be enslaved to an even greater extent than we are to myths and nostrums. On the other hand, in its search for the 'true' meaning of sex, in its intense interrogation of sexual difference, and in its obsessive categorization of sexual perversities it has contributed to the codification of a 'sexual tradition', a more or less coherent body of assumptions, beliefs, prejudices, rules, methods of investigation and forms of moral regulation, which still shape the way we live our sexualities. Is sex threatening and dangerous? If we want to believe that then we can find justification not only in a particular Christian tradition but in the writings also of the founding father of sexology, Krafft-Ebing, and in many of his scientific successors. Is sex, on the other hand, a source of potential freedom, whose liberatory power is only blocked by the regressive force of a corrupt civilization ('beneath the cobblestones the beach' as the student revolt in Paris, 1968, headily proclaimed)? If so, then justification can be found in works of polemicists and 'scientists' from the nineteenth century to the present, embracing not only socialist pioneers such as Charles Fourier and Edward Carpenter, Freudo-Marxists like Wilhelm Reich and Herbert Marcuse, but also more ostensibly sober-suited 'social bookkeepers' like Alfred Kinsey. Whatever our moral and political values, it has been difficult to escape the naturalistic fallacy that the key to our sex lies somewhere in the recesses of 'Nature', and that sexual science provides the best means of access to it. Not surprisingly, sexual theorists, as Murray Davis has noted, have become custodians of intellectual life, carrying out duties of guardianship and sanitation, tidying up the world by sweeping messy things into neat pigeonholes [6]. Unfortunately, the 'mess' keeps returning with the wind, endlessly confusing our gaze.

Against the certainties of this tradition I intend in this essay to offer an alternative way of understanding sexuality This involves seeing it not as a primordially 'natural' phenomenon but rather as a product of social and historical forces. 'Sexuality', I shall argue, is a 'fictional unity', that once did not exist, and at some time in the future may not exist again. It is an invention of the human mind. As Carole S. Vance has suggested, 'the most important organ in humans is located between the ears' [7].

This does not mean we can simply ignore the massive edifice of sexuality which envelops us. It has been argued that 'sexuality is without the importance ascribed to it in our contemporary society . . . it does not exist as such, because there is no such thing as sexuality' [8]. Here we see a reduction to absurdity of a valuable insight. Of course sexuality exists as a palpable social presence, shaping our personal and public lives. But I am suggesting that what we define as 'sexuality' is an historical construction, which brings together a host of different biological and mental possibilities — gender identity, bodily differences, reproductive capacities, needs, desires and fantasies — which need not be linked together, and in other cultures have not been. All the constituent elements of sexuality have their source either in the body or the mind, and I am not attempting to deny the limits posed by biology or mental processes. But the capacities of the body and the psyche are given meaning only in social relations. The next chapter, on 'The invention of sexuality' will attempt to justify this argument, while Chapters 3 and 4 will look at the implications of this approach for thinking about gender and sexual identities, and the fact of sexual diversity.

These chapters amount to a critique of what is now generally called the 'essentialist' approach to sex: that is a method which attempts to explain the properties of a complex whole by reference to a supposed inner truth or essence, the assumption 'that in all sexological matters there must be a single, basic, uniform pattern ordained by nature itself' [9]. This is, in the language of modern critical science, a *reductionist* method in that it reduces the complexity of the world to the imagined simplicities of its constituent units; and it is *deterministic* in that it seeks to explain individuals as automatic products of inner propulsions, whether of the genes, the instinct, the hormones, or the mysterious workings of the dynamic unconscious.

Against such an approach I shall argue that the meanings we give to 'sexuality' are socially organized, sustained by a variety of languages, which seek to tell us what sex is, what it ought to be — and what it could be. Existing languages of sex, embedded in moral treatises, laws, educational practices, psychological theories, medical definitions, social rituals, porno-graphic or romantic fictions, popular music, and commonsense assump-tions (most of which disagree) set the horizon of the possible. They all present themselves up as true representations of our intimate needs and desires. The difficulty lies in their contradictory appeals, in the babel of voices they bring forth. In order to make sense of them, and perhaps to go beyond the current limits on the possible, we need to learn to translate these languages — and to develop new ones. This has been one of the tasks of those who have sought, in recent years, to 'deconstruct' the apparent unity of this world of sexuality. Together they have provided the elements of a non-essentialist concept of 'sexuality'.

From social anthropology, sociology and post-Kinsey sex research there has come a growing awareness of the vast range of sexualities that exist in other cultures and within our own culture. Other cultures, Ruth Benedict noted, act as laboratories 'in which we may study the diversity of human institutions' [10]. An awareness that the way we do things is not the only way of living can provide a salutary jolt to our ethnocentricity. It can also force us to ask questions about why things are as they are today. Other cultures, and subcultures, are a mirror to our own transitoriness. Names of writers such as the anthropologists Malinowski or Mead, the biologist Kinsey or the sociologists Gagnon and Simon and Plummer recur in these pages because they tell us that variety not uniformity is the norm.

The legacy of Freud and his theory of the dynamic unconscious is another major source of the new sexual theory. From the tradition of psychoanalysis that he initiated has emerged a recognition that what goes on in the unconscious mind often contradicts the apparent certainties of conscious life. The life of the mind — of fantasies above all — reveals a diversity of desires to which the human being is heir. It unsettles the apparent solidities of gender, of sexual need, of identity. As Rosalind Coward has graphically said, 'In the private life of the mind, nothing is certain, nothing is fixed' [11].

Alongside these developments, the 'new social history' of recent years, with its emphasis on the history of populations and of 'mentalities', the experiences and beliefs of the downtrodden and oppressed as much as the powerful, has posed new questions about what we mean by 'the present' as well as about the 'history of the past'. *The History of Sexuality* by Michel Foucault has had a spectacular influence on modern thinking about sex because it grew out of, as well as contributed to, this fertile development of our historical understanding. Foucault, like Freud two generations earlier, stands at a crossroads of sexual thought, important as much for the questions he raises as for the answers he provides.

Finally, and most powerfully of all, the emergence of new social movements concerned with sex — modern feminism, the gay and lesbian and other radical sexual movements — have challenged many of the certainties of the 'sexual tradition', and have offered new insights into the intricate forms of power and domination that shape our sexual lives. The politics of homosexuality have placed on the agenda questions about sexual preference, identity, and choice. The women's movement has forced a recognition of the multiple forms of female sexual subordination, from endemic male violence and misogyny to sexual harassment and a pervasive language of sexual denigration and abuse. It has demanded a recognition of womens' rights over their own bodies by re-posing questions about consent and reproductive rights, desire and pleasure. Again there are as many questions posed as answers given. Differences have emerged between men and women, homosexuals and heterosexuals, black and white. No acceptable codes of appropriate behaviour have been elaborated despite all the heated debates. But something much more valuable has happened. We are being forced to rethink what we understand by sexuality because of a growing awareness of the tangled web of influences and forces — economics, race, gender, morals — that shape our emotions, needs, desires and relationships.

So what does a non-essentialist theory of sexuality mean for the politics of sexuality and for sexual ethics? These are the topics I examine in Chapters 5 and 6. They pose perhaps the most difficult challenges of all. The 'sexual tradition' assumed that your sex was your fate or destiny: what you desired was what you were. Sexuality pinned you down like a butterfly to the table. If you break with this tradition, if you reject the idea that sexuality embodies its own values and goals, then you are faced with complex problems of alignment and choice. Confronted by such uncertainties, it is all too easy to retreat into moral or political absolutes, to reassert again, against all the odds, against all the evidence, that there is a true sexuality that we must find at all costs. The aim of this essay is to challenge such absolutes without falling into the trap of saying no values are possible, 'anything goes'. 'Sexuality' is a deeply problematic concept, and there are no easy answers to the challenges it poses. But if we begin to ask the correct questions then we might find the way through the maze. We shall not find at the end of the journey a prescription for correct behaviour. But we might find a framework which allows us to come to terms with diversity — and to re-find, in sexuality, new opportunities for creative relationships, agency and choice.

REFERENCES

[1] Murray S. Davis, *Smut: Erotic Reality/Obscene Ideology,* University of Chicago Press, Chicago and London (1983), p. 87.

[2] Sue Cartledge, 'Duty and desire: creating a feminist morality' in Sue Cartledge and Joanna Ryan (eds.), *Sex and Love. New Thoughts on Old Contradictions,* The Women's Press, London (1983), p. 170.

[3] Michel Foucault, *The History of Sexuality,* Vol. I. *An Introduction,* trans. Robert Hurley, Allen Lane, London (1979).

[4] The terms are discussed in Raymond Williams, *Keywords. A Vocabulary of Culture and Society,* Flamingo, London (1983), pp. 283–286.

[5] Sigmund Freud, 'Introductory lectures on psychoanalysis', Lecture 21, in James Strachey (ed.), *The Standard Edition of the Complete Psychological Works of Sigmund Freud,* Vol. 16, Hogarth Press and the Institute of Psychoanalysis, London, 24 volumes (1953–1974), p. 323.

[6] Murray S. Davis, *op. cit.,* p. 272, note 1.

[7] *Diary of a Conference on Sexuality,* Barnard Women's Center (1982); Carole S. Vance, 'Pleasure and danger: towards a politics of sexuality', in Carole S. Vance (ed.), *Pleasure and Danger. Exploring Female Sexuality,* Routledge & Kegan Paul, Boston and London (1984).

[8] Stephen Heath, *The Sexual Fix,* Macmillan, London (1982), p. 3.

[9] Irving Singer, *The Goals of Human Sexuality,* Wildwood House, London (1973), p. 15.

[10] Ruth Benedict, *Patterns of Culture,* Routledge & Kegan Paul, London (1980, first published 1935), p. 12.

[11] Rosalind Coward, *Female Desire. Women's Sexuality Today,* Paladin, London (1984), p. 204.

2

The invention of sexuality

> . . . sexuality may be thought about, experienced, and acted on differently
> according to age, class, ethnicity, physical ability, sexual orientation and
> preference, religion, and region.
>
> Carole S. Vance [1]

A BRIEF HISTORY OF THE HISTORY OF SEXUALITY

When I first began writing about the history of sexuality I was fond of using
a phrase from the American historian, Vern Bullough: that sex in history
was a 'virgin field' [2]. This may have been a dubious pun but it was useful in
underlining an important, if often overlooked, reality. 'Sexuality' was
much talked about and written about but our historical knowledge about it
remained pretty negligible. Those would-be colonizers who ventured into
the field tended either to offer transcultural generalizations ('the history of
a long warfare between the dangerous and powerful drives and the systems
of taboos and inhibitions which man has erected to control them') [3] or to
subsume the subject under more neutral and acceptable labels ('marriage'
and 'morals' especially). Sex seemed marginal to the broad acres of
orthodox history.

Over the past decade or so much has changed, sometimes dramatically.
There has been a minor explosion of historical writings about sex. We now
know a great deal about such topics as marriage and the family, prostitution
and homosexuality, the forms of legal and medical regulation, pre-
Christian and non-Christian moral codes, women's bodies and health,
illegitimacy and birth control, rape and sexual violence, the evolution of
sexual identities and the importance of social networks and oppositional
sexualities. Historians have deployed sophisticated methods of family
reconstitution and demographic history, have intensively searched for new,
or interrogated old, documentary sources and made fuller use of oral

history interviews to reconstruct the subjective or the tabooed experience. Encouraged by a vigorous grass roots history, fed particularly by the impact of modern feminism and gay and lesbian politics, there is now an impressive library of articles, pamphlets and books. The history of sexuality may not yet be a respectable field of enquiry: sex research, as the sociologist Ken Plummer has noted, still makes you 'morally suspect' [4]. But it now at least has a degree of professional recognition and an interested, sometimes passionate, audience. It no longer seems quite such a bizarre and marginal activity as it once did. There is even a dawning recognition that it just might throw light on our confusing and confused present.

But having said this, we are still left with a dilemma — as to what exactly our object of study is. I can list, as I did above, a number of activities that we conventionally designate as sexual; but what is it that connects them? What is the magic element that defines some things as sexual and others not? At the heart of our concern, clearly, is an interest in the relations between men and women. One particular form of their interaction is the process of biological and social reproduction. No historian of sex would dare to ignore that. But a history of reproduction is not a history of sex. As Alfred Kinsey bitingly observed:

> Biologists and psychologists who have accepted the doctrine that the only natural function of sex is reproduction have simply ignored the existence of sexual activity which is not reproductive. They have assumed that heterosexual responses are a part of an animal's innate, 'instinctive' equipment, and that all other types of sexual activity represent 'perversions' of the 'normal instincts'. Such interpretations are, however, mystical. [5]

Most erotic interaction, even between those we easily call 'heterosexual', does not lead to procreation. And there are many forms of non-hetero-sexual sex, amongst women, and amongst men. Some of these patterns involve intercourse of one sort or another. Others do not. Most have at least the potentiality of leading to orgasm. Yet some activities which are clearly sex-related (for example transvestism) may lead to only chance 'sexual release' or none at all. Not even intimacy seems a clear enough criterion for judging what is sexual. Some activities we quite properly describe as sexual (masturbation) do not, on the surface at least, involve any other person at all; some aspects of intimacy have nothing to do with sex (and some sex is not intimate). Modern sociobiologists who wish to explain every manifestation of social life by reference to the 'timeless energy of the selfish genes' may see some biological logic in all of these activities. The rest of us, wisely in my opinion, are probably a little more sceptical. We are rather more than the 'survival machines — robots blindly programmed to preserve the molecule' that the sociobiologist Richard Dawkins describes [6].

So what is a history of sexuality a history of? My rather disappointing answer would be that it is a history without a proper subject; or rather as Robert Padgug has suggested, a history of a subject in constant flux [7]. It is often as much a history of *our* changing preoccupations about how we should live, how we should enjoy or deny our bodies, as about the past. The way we write about our sexuality tells us as much about the present and its concerns as about this past.

We are not, of course, the first generation to speculate about the history of sexuality, nor the first to be so revealing about our preoccupations in doing so. Some sense of the past has always been an important element for those that have been thinking about the meaning and implications of erotic life. In her book *Patriarchal Precedents,* Rosalind Coward has described the complex and heated debates in the last half of the nineteenth century about the nature of contemporary family and sexual forms [8]. Pioneering social scientists saw in sexuality a privileged site for speculations on the very origins of human society. From this flowed conflicting theories about the evolution and development of the various patterns of sexual life. Had the modern family evolved from the primitive clan, or was it already there, 'naturally', at the birth of history? Did our ancestors live in a state of primitive promiscuity, or was monogamy a biological necessity and fact? Was there once an Eden of sexual egalitarianism before the 'world historical defeat of the female sex', or was patriarchal domination present from the dawn of culture? On the resolution of such debates depended attitudes not only to existing social forms (marriage, sexual inequality, the double standard of morality) but also to other, 'primitive' cultures that existed contemporaneously with the Western. Could we find clues to our own evolutionary history in the rites and behaviours of the aborigines, stunted on the ladder of progress? Or did these people tell us something else about the variability of cultures?

We have still not fully escaped the effects of these evolutionist controversies. For much of this century racist practices have been legitimized by reference to the primitive condition of other races. Even those who extol the virtues of the sexual freedom of non-industrial societies rely on a belief that their peoples are somehow 'closer to nature'. Similarly, many of the contemporary feminist debates about the permanence of patriarchal male domination re-till the ground so feverishly worked over a century ago. Yet from the 1920s the older questions about the evolution of human culture were being displaced by a new anthropological approach, which asked different questions about sexuality.

This was associated in the first place with writers such as Bronislaw Malinowski and Margaret Mead. They recognized the danger of trying to understand our own pre-history by looking at existing societies. As a result, there was a new effort to try to understand each particular society in its own terms. This gave rise to a kind of cultural relativism in looking at other sexual mores, and a recognition of the validity of different sexual systems, however exotic they may have looked by the standards of twentieth-century industrial societies. This new approach was highly influential in helping to put Western culture, with all its discontents, into some sort of context. Moreover, by recognizing the diversity of sexual patterns all over the world, it contributed to a more sympathetic understanding of the diversity of sexual forms within our own culture. Social anthropology helped to provide a critical standard by which we could begin to judge the historical nature of our own society. The most famous example of this genre, Margaret Mead's romantic picture of 'coming of age' in Samoa, was enormously influential in the 1930s in large part because it demonstrated that the (repressive) American way of dealing with the problem of adolescence was neither desirable, inevitable, nor necessary [9].

There were, however, difficulties. On the one hand, there was the danger of attempting to understand all sexual acts by their function, as finely tuned responses to the claims of society. For Malinowski a grasp of the laws of society needed to be matched by a scientific understanding of the laws of nature, and he paid homage to Ellis and gave critical respect to Freud for helping him to grasp 'the universally human and fundamental' [10]. Malinowski saw cultures as delicate mechanisms designed to satisfy a basic human nature; in the process, the status of 'the natural' was not so much questioned as reaffirmed, though now it was less a product of evolution and more of basic instinctual needs. On the other hand, the endorsement of an 'infinite plasticity' of human needs by Ruth Benedict, Margaret Mead and their followers led not to a more historical account of sexual patterns but to a purely descriptive anthropology in which readers were offered wonderful, shimmering, evocations of the sexual lives of other peoples, but little sense of why these patterns were as they were. In the absence of any theory of determinative structures, again essentialist assumptions surreptitiously reasserted themselves.

The originality of contemporary attempts to develop a historical approach to sexuality lies in their willingness to question the naturalness and inevitability of the sexual categories and assumptions we have inherited. The sociologists Gagnon and Simon have talked of the need which may have existed at some unspecified time in the past to *invent* an importance for sexuality — perhaps because of underpopulation and threats of cultural submergence [11]. The French philosopher Michel Foucault has gone further by attempting to query the very category of 'sexuality' itself:

> Sexuality must not be thought of as a kind of natural given which power tries to hold in check, or as an obscure domain which knowledge tries gradually to uncover. It is the name that can be given to a historical construct. [12]

Foucault's work has made a vital contribution to recent discussions on the history of sexuality precisely because it burst onto and grew out of work that was creatively developing in sociology and in radical social history. It helped to give a focus for questions already being formed. To questions about what shaped sexual beliefs and behaviours, a new one was added, concerning the history of the idea of sexuality itself. For Foucault, sexuality was a relationship of elements, a series of meaning giving practices and activities, a social apparatus which had a history — with complex roots in the pre-Christian and Christian past, but achieving a modern conceptual unity, with diverse effects, only within the modern world.

The most important result of this historical approach to sexuality is that it opens the whole field to critical analysis and assessment. It becomes possible to relate sexuality to other social phenomena. Three types of question then become critically important. First: how is sexuality shaped, how is it articulated with economic, social and political structures, in a phrase, how is it 'socially constructed'? Second: how and why has the domain of sexuality achieved such a critical organizing and symbolic significance in Western culture; why do we think it is so important? Third: what is the relationship between sex and power; what role should we assign class divisions, patterns of male domination and racism? Coursing through each of these questions is a recurrent preoccupation: if sexuality is constructed by human agency, to what extent can it be changed? This is the question I shall attempt to deal with in succeeding chapters. The first three I shall examine in turn in the rest of this chapter.

THE 'SOCIAL CONSTRUCTION' OF SEXUALITY

The commonly used term 'the social construction of sexuality' has a harsh and mechanistic sound. But at its heart is a quite straightforward concern, with 'the intricate and multiple ways in which our emotions, desires and relationships are shaped by the society we live in' [13].

In practice, most writers on our sexual past assume that sex is an irresistible natural energy barely held in check by a thin crust of civilization. For Malinowski:

> Sex is a most powerful instinct . . . there is no doubt that masculine jealousy, sexual modesty, female coyness, the mechanism of sexual attraction and of courtship — all these forces and conditions made it necessary that even in the most primitive human aggregates there should exist powerful means of regulating, suppressing and directing this instinct.

'Sex', as he put it in another paper, 'really is dangerous', the source of most human trouble from Adam and Eve onwards [14].

In these words we can still hear echoes of Krafft-Ebing's view at the end of the nineteenth century of sex as an all-powerful instinct which demands fulfilment against the claims of morals, belief and social restrictions. But even more orthodox academic historians speak in rather similar language. Lawrence Stone, for instance, in *The Family, Sex and Marriage* sensibly rejects the idea that 'the id' (the energy of the Freudian unconscious) is the most powerful and unchanging of all drives. He suggests that changes in protein, in diet, in physical exertion and in psychic stress all have an effect on the organization of sex. Yet he still speaks of 'the super ego' (our internalized system of values) at times repressing and at other times releasing sexual drive, which eloquently reproduces the very old traditional picture [15].

These approaches assume that sex offers a basic 'biological mandate' which presses against and must be restrained by the cultural matrix. This is what I mean by an essentialist approach to sexuality. It takes many forms. Liberatory theorists such as Reich and Marcuse tend to see sex as a beneficient force which is repressed by a corrupt civilization. Contemporary sociobiologists on the other hand see all social forms as in some unspecified way emanations of basic genetic material. Yet they all see a world of nature which provides the raw material we must use for the understanding of the social. Against all these arguments I want to stress that sexuality is shaped by social forces. And far from being the most natural element in social life, the most resistant to cultural moulding, it is perhaps one of the most susceptible to organization. Indeed I would go so far as to say that sexuality only exists through its social forms and social organization. Moreover, the forces that shape and mould the erotic possibilities of the body vary from society to society. 'Sexual socialization', Ellen Ross and Rayner Rapp have written, 'is no less specific to each culture than is socialization to ritual, dress or cuisine' [16]. This puts the emphasis firmly where it should belong, on society and social relations rather than on nature.

I do not wish to deny the importance of biology. The physiology and morphology of the body provides the preconditions for human sexuality. Biology conditions and limits what is possible. But it does not cause the patterns of sexual life. We cannot reduce human behaviour to the mysterious workings of the DNA or what two contemporary writers have recently called 'the dance of the chromosomes' [17]. I prefer to see in biology a set of potentialities which are transformed and given meaning only in social relationships. Human consciousness and human history are very complex phenomena.

This theoretical stance has many roots: in the sociology and anthropology of sex, in the revolution in psychoanalysis and in the new social history. But despite these disparate starting points, it coheres around a number of common assumptions. First, there is a general rejection of sex as an autonomous realm, a natural domain with specific effects, a rebellious energy that the social controls. We can no longer set 'sex' against 'society' as if they were separate domains. Secondly, there is a widespread recognition of the social variability of sexual forms, beliefs, ideologies and behaviour. Sexuality has a history, or more realistically, many histories, each of which needs to be understood both in its uniqueness and as part of an intricate pattern. Thirdly, we must abandon the idea that we can fruitfully understand the history of sexuality in terms of a dichotomy of pressure and release, repression and liberation. Sexuality is not a head of steam that must be capped lest it destroy us; nor is it a life force we must release to save our civilization. Instead we must learn to see that sexuality is something which society produces in complex ways. It is a result of diverse social practices that give meaning to human activities, of social definitions and self-definitions, of struggles between those who have power to define and regulate, and those who resist. Sexuality is not given, it is a product of negotiation, struggle and human agency.

Nothing is sexual, Plummer has suggested, but naming makes it so [18]. If this is the case it follows that we need to move gingerly in applying our Western definitions to other cultures. Both the significance attributed to sexuality and attitudes to the various manifestations of erotic life vary enormously. Some societies display so little interest in erotic activity that they have been labelled more or less 'asexual' [19]. Islamic cultures, by contrast, have developed a lyrical view of sex with sustained attempts at integrating the religious and the sexual. Bouhdiba writes of 'the radical legitimacy of the practice of sexuality' in the Islamic world — as long, that is, as it was not homosexual, 'violently condemned' by Islam [20]. The Christian West, notoriously, has seen in sex a terrain of moral anguish and conflict, setting up an enduring dualism between the spirit and the flesh, the mind and the body. It has had the inevitable result of creating a cultural configuration which simultaneously disavows the body while being obsessively preoccupied with it.

Within the wide parameters of general cultural attitudes, each culture labels different practices as appropriate or inappropriate, moral or immoral, healthy or perverted. Western culture continues to define appropriate behaviour in terms of a limited range of acceptable activities. Monogamous marriage between partners of roughly equal age but different genders remains the norm (though not, of course, necessarily the reality) and, despite many changes, the accepted gateway to adulthood, and sexual activity. Homosexuality, on the other hand, carries a heavy legacy of taboo. Homosexuals may be accepted today, Dennis Altman has remarked, but homosexuality is not, and in a climate where a disease like AIDS can lead to a press panic about gay lifestyles, this rings true [21]. Other cultures have not found it necessary to issue the same injunction. The anthropologists Ford and Beach found that only 15 per cent of 185 different societies surveyed restricted sexual liaisons to single mateships. Kinsey's figures suggested that beneath a surface conformity Western practices are as varied: in his 1940s sample, 50 per cent of males and 26 per cent of females had extra-marital sex by the age of 40 [22].

Marriage is not inevitably heterosexual — amongst the Nuer, older women 'marry' younger women [23]. Nor is homosexuality universally tabooed. There are various forms of institutionalized homosexuality, from puberty rites in African tribes, to pedagogic relations between older men and youths (as in Ancient Greece), to the integrated transvestite partnerships (the berdache) among native Americans [24].

We in the West still define the norms of sex in relationship to one of the possible results — reproduction. For long centuries of Christian dominance it was *the only* justification of sexual relations. Other cultures, however, have sometimes failed even to make the connection between copulation and procreation. Some societies only recognize the role of the father, others the mother. The Trobriand Islanders investigated by Malinowski saw no connection between intercourse and reproduction. It was only *after* the spirit child entered the womb that intercourse assumed any significance for them, in moulding the character of the future child [25].

Each culture makes what Plummer calls 'who restrictions' and 'how restrictions'. 'Who restrictions' are concerned with the gender of the partners, the species, age, kin, race, caste or class which limit who we may take as partners. 'How restrictions' have to do with the organs that we use, the orifices we may enter, the manner of sexual involvement and sexual intercourse: what we may touch, when we may touch, with what frequency, and so on [26]. These regulations take many forms: formal and informal, legal and extra-legal. They tend not to apply in an undifferentiated way for the whole of society. For instance, there are usually different rules for men and women, shaped in ways which subordinate women's sexuality to men's. These rules are often more acceptable as abstract norms than as practical guides. But they provide the permissions, prohibitions, limits and possibilities through which erotic life is constructed.

Five broad areas stand out as being particularly crucial in the social organization of sexuality: kinship and family systems, economic and social organization, social regulation, political interventions, and the development of 'cultures of resistance'.

(1) Kinship and family systems

These *appear* as the most basic and unchanging forms of all — pre-eminently the 'natural' focus of sexual socialization and experience. The taboo on incest, that is the prohibition of sexual involvement within certain degrees of relationship, seems to be a universal law, marking the passage, it has been often argued, from a state of nature to human society: it is constitutive of culture. (It is also the basis for our most enduring myth — that of Oedipus.) Yet the forms of the taboo vary enormously. In the Christian traditions of the Middle Ages, marriage to the seventh degree of relationship was prohibited. Today, marriage to first cousins is allowed. In the Egypt of the Pharoahs, sibling marriages were permitted, and in some cases so were father–daughter marriages, in the interests of preserving the purity of the royal line [27]. The existence of the incest taboo illustrates the need of all societies to regulate sex — but not how it is done. Even 'blood relationships' have to be interpreted through the grid of culture.

The truth is that kin ties are not *natural* links of blood but are social relations between groups, often based on residential affinities and hostile to genetic affinities. Marshall Sahlins has argued that:

> human conceptions of kinship may be so far from biology as to exclude all but a small fraction of a person's genealogical connections from the category of 'close kin', while at the same time, including in that category, as sharing common blood, very distantly related people or even complete strangers. Among these strangers (genetically) may be one's own children (culturally).[28]

Who we decide are kin and what we describe as 'the family' are clearly dependent on a range of historical factors. There are many different family forms especially within highly industrialized, Western societies — between different classes, and different geographic, religious, racial and ethnic groups. Family patterns are shaped and re-shaped by economic factors, by rules of inheritance, by state interventions to regulate marriage and divorce or to support the family by social welfare or taxation policies. All these affect the likely patterns of sexual life: by encouraging or discouraging the rate of marriage, age of marriage, incidence of reproduction, attitudes to non-procreative or non heterosexual sex, the relative power of men over women, and so on. These factors are important in themselves. They are doubly important because the family is the arena in which most of us in Western culture gain some sense of our individual sexual needs and identities, and if we follow psychoanalysis, it is the arena where our desires are organized from a very early stage indeed. So to understand sexuality we have to understand much more than sex: we have to understand the relationships in which most of it takes place.

(2) Economic and social organization

As I have suggested, families themselves are not autonomous, natural entities. They themselves are shaped by wider social relations. Domestic patterns can be changed by economic forces, by the class divisions to which economic change gives rise, by the degree of urbanization and of rapid industrial and social change [29]. In the past, and probably also in the present, labour migrations have affected patterns of courtship and have helped dictate the incidence of illegitimacy rates. The proletarianization of the rural population in early nineteenth-century England helped to contribute to the massive rise of illegitimacy during this period as old courtship patterns were broken by economic and industrial dislocation — a case of 'marriage frustrated' rather than a conscious sexual revolution. Work conditions can shape sexual lives. A good example of this is provided by the evidence for the 1920s and 1930s that women who worked in factories tended to be much more familiar with methods of artificial birth control, and thus to limit their family size to a greater degree than women who worked solely in the home or in domestic service [30].

The relations between men and women are constantly affected by changes in economic conditions. The growing involvement of married women in the paid workforce in the 1950s and 1960s inevitably affected the patterns of domestic life. It also fuelled a consumer boom which provided one of the preconditions for a proliferation of new markets for sexual commodities in the past generation. Sexuality is not *determined* by the mode of production, but the rhythms of economic life provide the basic preconditions and ultimate limits for the organization of sexual life.

(3) Social regulation

If economic life establishes some of the fundamental rhythms, the actual forms of regulation of sexuality have a considerable autonomy. Formal methods of regulating sexual life vary from time to time depending on the significance of religion, the changing role of the state, the existence or not of a moral consensus which regulate marriage patterns, divorce rates and incidence of sexual unorthodoxy. One of the critical shifts of the last hundred years has been the move away from moral regulation by the churches to a more secular mode of organization through medicine, education, psychology, social work and welfare practices. It is also import-ant to recognize that the effects of these interventions are not necessarily pre-ordained. As often as not sexual life is altered by the unintended consequences of social action as much as the intention of the authors. Laws banning obscene publications more often than not give rise to court cases that publicize them. Banning sexy films give them a fame they might not otherwise deserve. More seriously, laws designed to control the behaviour of certain groups of people can actually give rise to an enhanced sense of identity and cohesion amongst them. This certainly seems to be the case with the refinement of the laws relating to male homosexuality in the late nineteenth century [31].

But it is not only formal methods which shape sexuality; there are many informal and customary patterns which are equally important. The traditio-nal forms of regulation of adolescence courtship can be critical means of social control. It is very difficult to break with the consensus of one's village or one's peer group in school, and this is as much true today as it was in the pre-industrial societies. A language of sexual abuse ('slags' and 'sluts') works to keep girls in line, and to enforce conventional distinctions between girls who do and girls who don't. Such informal methods enforced by strictly adhered to rules often produce, by contemporary standards, various bizarre manifestations of sexual behaviour. One such example is provided by the traditional form of courtship in parts of England and Wales up to the nineteenth century known as 'bundling', which involved intimate but fully clothed rituals of sex play in bed. Closer to the present, we can find the equally exotic phenomenon of petting, which is dependent on the belief that while intercourse in public is tabooed, other forms of play, because they are not defined as *the* sex act, may be intimately engaged in. Kinsey noted in the early 1950s that:

> Foreign travellers are sometimes amazed at the open display of
> such obviously erotic activity . . . There is an increasing amount

of petting which is carried on in such public conveyances as buses, trams, and airplanes. The other passengers have learned to ignore such activities if they are pursued with some discretion. Orgasm is sometimes achieved in the petting which goes on in such public places. [32]

Implicit in such phenomena are intricate though only semiconscious rules which limit what can and cannot be done. Informal methods of regulation like these can have important social effects — in limiting, for example, illegitimate conceptions. They have often been enforced in the past by customary patterns of public shaming, rituals of humiliation and public mocking — examples include the 'charivari' and 'rough music' — which serve to reinforce the norms of the community.

(4)   Political interventions
These formal and informal methods of control exist within a changing political framework. The balance of political forces at any particular time can determine the degree of legislative control or moral intervention in sexual life. The general social climate provides the context in which some issues take on a greater significance than others. The existence of skilled 'moral entrepeneurs' able to articulate and call up inchoate currents of opinion can be decisive in enforcing existing legislation or in conjuring up new. The recent success of the New Right in America in establishing an agenda for sexual conservatism by mobilizing against sexual liberals and/or sexual deviants underlines the possibilities of political mobilization around sex.

(5)   Cultures of resistance
But the history of sexuality is not a simple history of control, it is also a history of opposition and resistance to moral codes. Forms of moral regulation give rise to cultures of resistance. A prime example of these is provided by the female networks of knowledge about methods of birth control especially abortion. As Angus McLaren has put it:

> In studying abortion beliefs it is possible to glimpse aspects of a separate female sexual culture that supports the independence and autonomy of women from medical men, moralists and spouses.

There is a long history of such alternative knowledge. A classic example is provided by the widespread use of the lead compound diachylon in the late nineteenth century and early twentieth century in the Midlands of England. Widely used as an antiseptic, it was accidentally discovered that this could be used to induce abortions and there is evidence of its subsequent spread as a prophylactic amongst working-class women up to the outbreak of the First World War [33].

Other examples of cultural resistance come from the emergence of the subcultures and networks established by sexual minorities. There is a long history of subcultures of male homosexuality throughout the history of the West, manifest for instance in Italian towns of the late Middle Ages, and in England from the late seventeenth century. These have been critical for the emergence of modern homosexual identities which have been largely formed in these wider social networks. More recently, over the last hundred years or so, there have been series of explicit oppositional political movements organized around sexuality and sexual issues. The classic example is that of feminism. But in addition recent historical work has demonstrated the longstanding existence of sex reform movements often closely linked to campaigns for homosexual rights: the modern gay and lesbian movements have antecedents going back to the nineteenth century in countries like Germany and Britain [34].

What we so confidently know as 'sexuality' is, then, a product of many influences and social interventions. It does not exist outside history but is a historical product. This is what we mean by 'the social construction' of sexuality.

THE IMPORTANCE OF SEX

All societies have to make arrangements for the organization of erotic life. Not all, however, do it with the same obsessive concern as the West. Throughout the history of the West, since the time of the Ancient Greeks, what we call sexuality has been an object of moral concern, but the concept of sexual life has not been the same. For the Ancient Greeks concern with the pleasures of the body — *aphrodisia* — was only one, and not necessarily the most important of the preoccupations of life to be set alongside dietary regulations and the organization of household relations. And the object of debate was quite different too. Freud, with his usual perceptiveness, was able to sum up one aspect of this difference:

> The most striking distinction between the erotic life of antiquity and our own no doubt lies in the fact that the ancients laid the

stress upon the instinct itself, whereas we emphasise its object.
[35]

We are preoccupied *with whom* we have sex, the ancients with the question of excess or over-indulgence, activity and passivity. Plato would have banned pederasty from his city not because it was against nature, but because it was in excess of what nature demands. Sodomy was excessively licentious, and the moral question was not whether you had sex with a man if you were a man, but whether you were active or passive. Passive homosexual practices and the people who practised them were rejected not for homosexuality but for passivity [36]. We, on the other hand, have been obsessively concerned whether a person is normal or abnormal, defined in terms of whether we are heterosexual or homosexual. We seek the truth of our natures in our sexual desires. This represents a major shift in the organizing significance given to sexuality.

This is the product of a long and complicated history. But there seem to be three key moments in its evolution. The first came with innovations of the first century A.D., before the generalized advent of a Christianized West. It was represented by a new austerity and by a growing disapproval of *mollities,* that is, sex indulged in purely for pleasure. The Church accepted and refined the view that husbands should not behave incontinently with wives in marriage. The purpose of sex was reproduction, so sex outside marriage was obviously for pleasure and hence a sin. As Flandrin has said, 'marriage was a kind of preventive medicine given by God to save man from immorality' [37]. The sins of the flesh were a constant temptation from the divine path.

The second crucial moment came in the twelfth and thirteenth centuries after a series of intense critical and religious struggles with the triumph of the Christian tradition of sex and marriage. This did not necessarily affect everyone's behaviour in society. What it did do was to establish a new norm which was enforced by both the religious and the secular arm. Marriage was a matter of family arrangement for the good of families. So for two people thrown together often as strangers, a tight set of rules had to be elaborated. As a result, 'the couple were not alone in their marriage bed: the shadow of the confessor loomed over their frolics' [38]. Theologians and canonists discussed the sex lives of married couples to the last detail, not simply as an intellectual game but to provide detailed answers to practical moral questions.

The third crucial, and decisive, moment occurred in the eighteenth and nineteenth centuries with the increasing definition of sexual normality in terms of relations with the opposite sex, and the consequent categorization of other forms as deviant. This last change is the one of which we are immediate heirs. It was represented by a shift from religious organization of moral life to increasingly secular regulation embodied in the emergence of new medical, psychological and educational norms. Alongside this, new typologies of degeneracy and perversion emerged and there was a decisive growth of new sexual indentities. Homosexuality moved from being a category of sin to become a psychosocial disposition. Sexology began to speculate about the laws of sex and 'sexuality' finally emerged as a separate continent of knowledge with its own distinct effects.

The emergence of the category of homosexuality and 'the homosexual' illustrates what was taking place. Homosexual activities are of course widespread in all cultures and there is a sustained history of homosexuality in the West. But the idea that there is such a thing as *the* homosexual person is a relatively new one. All the evidence suggests that before the eighteenth century homosexuality, interpreted in its broadest sense as involving erotic activities between people of the same gender, certainly existed, 'homosexuals' did not. Certain acts such as sodomy were severly condemned: in Britain they carried the death penalty, formally at least, until 1861, but there seems to have been little idea of a distinct type of homosexual personage. Sodomy was not a specifically homosexual crime; the law applied indifferently to relations between men and women, men and beasts, as well as men and men. And while by the eighteenth century the persistent sodomite was clearly perceived as a special type of person, he was still defined by the nature of his act rather than the character of his personality. From the mid-nineteenth century, however, 'the homosexual' (the term 'homosexuality' was invented in the 1860s) was increasingly seen as belonging to a particular species of being, characterized by feelings, latency and a psychosexual condition. This view was elaborated by pioneering sexologists who produced ever more complex explanations and descriptions. Was homosexuality a product of corruption or degeneration, congenital or the result of childhood trauma? Was it a natural variation or a perverse deformation? Should it be tolerated or subjected to cure? Havelock Ellis distinguished the invert from the pervert, Freud the 'absolute invert', the 'amphigenic' and the 'contingent'. Rather later, Clifford Allen distinguished twelve types, ranging from the compulsive, the nervous, the neurotic and the psychotic to the psychopathic and the alcoholic. Kinsey invented a seven-point rating for the spectrum of heterosexual/homosexual behaviour, which allowed his successors to distinguish a 'Kinsey one' from a 'five' or 'six' as if real life depended upon it [39].

This labelling and pigeonholing energy and zeal has led a number of historians to argue that the emergence of distinct categories of sexual beings over the past century is the consequence of a sustained effort at social control. Writers on the history of lesbianism have suggested that the development of a sexualized lesbian identity at the end of the nineteenth century and early twentieth century was an imposition by sexologists designed precisely to split women from women, breaking the ties of emotionality and affection which bind all women together against men [40]. There is clearly an element of truth in this. Nevertheless I think it much more credible to see the emergence of distinct identities during this period as the product of struggle against prevailing norms, which had necessarily different effects for men and women. Sexologists did not so much invent the homosexual or the lesbian as attempt to put into their own characteristic pathologizing language changes that were taking place before their eyes. Pioneering sexologists like Krafft-Ebing were confronted by people appearing in the courts or coming to them for help largely as a result of a new politically motivated zeal to control all manifestations of sexual desire. The definition of homosexuality as a distinct perversion was one attempt to come to terms with this new reality. It produced an inevitable response in the urge to self-definition.

Sexual activity was increasingly coming to define a particular type of person. In return people were beginning to define themselves as different and their difference was constituted around their sexuality. One Thomas Newton was arrested in London in 1726, entrapped by a police informant in a homosexual act. Confronted by the police he said: 'I did it because I thought I knew him, and I think there is no crime in making what use I please of my own body' [41]. Here we can see, embryonically, the urge to self-definition that was to flourish in the proliferation of homosexual identities in the twentieth century. In turn, the growth of the category of the homosexual at the end of the nineteenth century presaged a profusion of new sexual types and identities in the twentieth century: the transvestite, the transsexual, the bisexual, the paedophile, the sado-masochist and so on. Increasingly in the twentieth century people have defined themselves by defining their sex. The question we have to ask is why sexuality has become so central to our definition of self and of normality.

Sexuality is shaped at the juncture of two major axes of concern: with our subjectivity — who and what we are; and with society — with the future growth, well-being, health and prosperity of the population as a whole. The two are intimately connected because at the heart of both is the body and its potentialities. 'As the human body becomes autonomous and self-conscious', Lowe has written, that is, as it becomes the object of a fully secular attention:

as emotion recoiled from the world and became more cooped up, sexuality in bourgeois society emerged as an explicit phenomenon. [42]

And as society has become more and more concerned with the lives of its members, for the sake of moral uniformity, economic well-being, national security or hygiene and health, so it has become more and more preoccupied with the sex lives of its individuals, giving rise to intricate methods of administration and management, to a flowering of moral anxieties, medical, hygienic, legal and welfarist interventions, or scientific delving, all designed to understand the self by understanding sex.

Sexuality as a result has become an increasingly important social and political as well as moral issue. If we look at all the major crises in Britain since the beginning of the nineteenth century we see that in one way or another a preoccupation with sex has been integral to them. In the crisis of the French revolutionary wars in the early nineteenth century one of the central preoccupations of ideologists was with the moral decline which it was believed had set off the train of events leading to the collapse of the French monarchy. In the 1830s and 1840s, with the first crisis of the new industrial society, there was an obsessive concern with the sexuality of women and the threat to children who worked in the factories and mines. By the mid-nineteenth century, attempts to re-order society focused on the question of moral hygiene and health. From the 1860s to the 1890s prostitution, the moral standards of society and moral reform were at the heart of public debate, many seeing in moral decay a sign of impending imperial decline. In the early decades of the twentieth century these concerns were re-ordered in a new concern with the quality of the British population. The vogue for eugenics, the planned breeding of the best in society, though never dominant, had a significant influence in shaping both welfare policies and the attempt to re-order national priorities in the face of international competition. Inevitably it fed into a burgeoning racism during this century. During the inter-war years and into the 1940s, the decline of the birth-rate engendered fevered debates about the merits of birth control, selective encouragement of family planning policies, and the country falling into the hands of the once subject races. By the 1950s, in the period of the Cold War, there was a new searching out of sexual degenerates, especially homosexuals, because they were apparently curiously susceptible to treachery. This was to become a major aspect of the McCarthyite witch hunt in the USA which had echoes in Britain and elsewhere. By the 1980s in the wake of several decades of so-called permissiveness, minority forms of sexuality, especially homosexuality, were being blamed for the decline of the family and gave new energy to a revival of right wing political forces.

A series of concerns are crystallized in these crises: with the norms of family life, the relations between men and women, the nature of female sexuality, the question of sexual deviance, the relations between adults and children, and so on. These are critical issues in any society. The debates about them in Britain over the last few decades have been heated precisely because debates about sexuality are debates about the nature of society; as sex goes, so goes society.

SEXUALITY AND POWER

This is another way of saying that issues of sexuality are increasingly important in the whole working of power in contemporary society. I mentioned earlier that one of the effects of a historical approach to sexuality was to see power over sexuality as productive rather than negative or repressive. The metaphor of repression comes from hydraulics: it offers the image of a gushing energy that must be held in check. The historical approach to sexuality would stress rather the impact of various social practices that construct sexual regulations, give meaning to bodily activities, shape definitions and limit and control human behaviour.

The rejection of a repression model (what Foucault called the 'repressive hypothesis') does not of course mean that all regimes of sexual regulation are of equal force or effectiveness. Some are clearly more harsh, authoritarian and oppressive than others. One of the important results of the new historical investigation of sexuality has been a reassessment of the whole Victorian period. Classically this has been seen as a period of unique moral hypocrisy and sexual denial. It is now increasingly apparent that this is highly misleading. Far from witnessing an avoidance of sex, the nineteenth century was not far from being obsessesd with sexual issues. Rather than being the subject that was hidden away, it was a topic that was increasingly discussed in relation to diverse aspects of social life. This does not mean, however, that the Victorian period can now be seen as peculiarly liberal. In England the death penalty for sodomy was still on the statute book until 1861. Restrictions on female sexual autonomy were severe and the distinction between respectable women and the unregenerates (the virgin and the whore, the madonna and the magdalen) reached their apogee during this period. Although the present may not have produced a perfect resolution of all conflict, for many of us who live in it it is infinitely preferable to what existed a hundred years ago.

The usefulness of abandoning the repressive model, in its crude form, however, is that it does direct us towards an attempt to understand the actual mechanisms of power at work in any particular period. Power no longer appears a single entity which is held or controlled by a particular group, the state or the ruling class. It is, in Schur's phrase, 'more like a process than an object', [43] a malleable and mobile force which takes many different forms and is exercised through a variety of different social practices and relationships. If this approach to power is adopted then we need to abandon any theoretical approach which sees sexuality moulded by a dominant, determining will — whether it be of 'society', as functionalist sociology tended to suggest, or 'capitalism', as Marxists might argue, or 'patriarchy', as some feminists would propose. Power does not operate through single mechanisms of control. It operates through complex and overlapping — and often contradictory — mechanisms which produce domination *and* oppositions, subordination *and* resistances.

There are many structures of domination and subordination in the world of sexuality but three major axes seem peculiarly important today: those of class, of gender, and of race.

(1) Class

Class differences in sexual regulation are not unique to the modern world. In the slave-owning society of pre-Christian Rome, moral standards varied with social status. 'To be *impudicus* (that is passive) is disgraceful for a free man', wrote the elder Seneca, 'but it is the slave's absolute obligation towards his master, and the freed man owes a moral duty of compliance' [44]. What was true in the ancient world has become more sharply apparent in the modern. It has in fact been argued (by Foucault) that the very idea of 'sexuality' is an essentially bourgeois one, which developed as an aspect of the self-definition of a class, both against the decadent aristocracy and the rampant immorality of the lower orders in the course of the eighteenth and nineteenth centuries. It was a colonizing system of beliefs which sought to remould the polity in its own image. The respectable standards of family and domestic life, with the increased demarcations between male and female roles, a growing ideological distinction between private and public life, and a marked concern with moral and hygienic policing of non-marital, non-heterosexual sexuality, was increasingly the norm by which all behaviour was judged. This does not, of course, mean that all or even most behaviour conformed to the norm. There is plentiful evidence that the behaviour of the working classes remained extremely resilient to middle-class manners. Nevertheless, the complex sexual patterns that exist in the twentieth century are a product of a social struggle in which class was a vital element. This has resulted, not surprisingly, in distinct class patterns of sexual life. Kinsey's American sample of 18,000 in the 1940s suggested that whether it be on masturbation, homsexuality, the incidence of oral sex, petting, concourse with prostitutes, pre-marital or extra-marital sex, or 'total sexual outlet', there were significantly different class patterns amongst men. For women, on the other hand, class differences played a relatively minor part: their age and gender ideologies were much more critical factors in shaping behaviour. Later surveys, while taking note of the gradual erosion of class boundaries have confirmed the continuing existence of class sexualities. It is hardly surprising, then, that the literature abounds with images of relations between men and women (and indeed between men and men) where class, power and sexual desire are intricately interwoven.

(2)   Gender

Class, as we have seen, is not an undifferentiated category. Classes consist of men and women, and class and status differences may not have the same significance for women as for men. Gender is a crucial divide.

A number of feminist writers have seen the elaboration of sexual difference as crucial to the oppression of women, with sexuality not merely reflecting but being fundamental to the construction and maintenance of the power relations between women and men [45]. As a general statement this is clearly apt. The patterns of female sexuality are inescapably a product of the historically rooted power of men to define and categorize what is necessary and desirable. 'To be a woman', Rosalind Coward has said:

> is to be constantly addressed, to be constantly scrutinised . . .
> Female desire is crucial to our whole social structure. Small wonder it is so closely obscured, so endlessly pursued, so frequently recast and reformulated. [46]

And it is, of course, still pursued, recast and reformulated by men. As Richard Dyer has put it, male sexuality is a bit like air — 'you breathe it in all the time, but you aren't aware of it much' [47]. We look at the world through our concepts of male sexuality so that even when we are not looking at male sexuality as such we are looking at the world within its framework of reference.

It would be wrong, however, to see this power of definition as either monolithic or unchallenged. The law, medicine, even popular opinion is highly contradictory and changes over time. Before the eighteenth century female sexuality was regarded as voracious and all-consuming. In the nineteenth century there was a sustained effort to inform the population that female sexuality amongst respectable women just did not exist. In the twentieth century there has been a general incitement to female sexuality as an aid to all forms of consumerism. The sexuality of women has at various times been seen as dangerous, as a source of disease, as the means of transmitting national values in the age of eugenics, as the guardian of moral purity in debates over sex education, and as the main focus of attention in the debates over permissiveness and sexual liberation in the 1960s. Female sexuality has been limited by economic and social dependence, by the power of men to define sexuality, by the limitations of marriage, by the burdens of reproduction and by the endemic fact of male violence against women. At the same time, these contradictory definitions have as often provided the opportunity for women to define their own needs and desires. Since the late nineteenth century the acceptable spaces for self-definition have expanded rapidly to include not only pleasure in marriage but also relatively respectable forms of unmarried and non-procreative heterosexual activity. Yet, as Vance observes, gross and public departures from '"good" woman status' — such as lesbianism, promiscuity or non-traditional heterosexuality — still invite, and are used to justify, violation [48]. The patterns of male privilege have not been broken. At the same time, the real changes of this century and the continued vitality of feminism testify that these patterns are neither inevitable nor immutable.

(3) Race

Categorizations by class or gender intersect with those of ethnicity and race. Historians of sex have not actually ignored race in the past, but they have fitted it into their pre-existing framework. So the evolutionary model of sexuality put forward by the theorists of the late nineteenth century inevitably presented the black person — 'the savage' — as lower down the evolutionary scale than the white, as closer to nature. This view survived even in the culturally relativist and apparently liberal writings of Margaret Mead. One of the attractions of her portrayal of Samoan life was precisely the idea that Samoans were in some indefinable sense freer of constraints and closer to nature than contemporary Americans. The most abiding myth is that of the insatiability of the sexual needs of non-European peoples and the threat they consequently pose for the purity of the white race. A fear of black male priapism, and the converse exploitation of black women to service their masters, was integral to slave society in the American South in the nineteenth century and has survived in a series of stereotypes in the twentieth century. In apartheid South Africa the prohibitions of the Mixed Marriages Act and section 16 of the Immorality Act designed to prevent miscegenation were among the first pieces of apartheid legislation to be introduced after the National Party came to power on a policy of racial segregation in 1948. As the regime attempted to deal with the crisis of apartheid in the 1980s by reshaping its forms, one of the first pillars of arpartheid it attempted to remove were precisely these acts. As a result the regime came under heavy criticism from extreme right wing groups which argued that the whole edifice of apartheid would be undermined if the laws were repealed. On a global scale, the belief in the superiority of European norms is perhaps most clearly revealed in the obsessive Western concern with the population explosion of the Third World, which has led to various efforts on the part of development agencies as well as local authorities to impose Western patterns of artificial birth control, sometimes with disastrous results as the delicate ecology of social life has been unbalanced. It should serve to remind us that modern attitudes to birth control are rooted both in women's desire to limit their own fertility and also in a eugenic and 'family planning' policy whose aim was the survival and fitness of the European races. Elements of this eugenicist past are common in current practices. In Israel Jewish families receive higher child allowances than Arab ones, while in Britain the dangerous contraceptive injection, Depo Provera, has been given virtually exclusively to black and very poor women. One study has even found more birth control leaflets in family planning clinics in Asian languages than in English. Behind all such examples is the assumption that there is an appropriate civilized norm of sexual behaviour to which all people have to bend a knee. This belief in turn is encoded in a series of practices, from immigration laws to birth control propaganda, from medical attitudes to the pathologizing in psychology and sociology of different patterns of family life [49].

It is not surpising, then, that many black and ethnic minority peoples in both Western countries and the Third World reject the analyses of contemporary feminist and radical sexual politics as being irretrievably shaped by more or less unconscious racist beliefs. This has led to the exposition and development of forms of sexual politics which are particular to the experience of black people and simultaneously engaged with anti-racist politics.

The boundaries of race, gender and class inevitably overlap. Black people in Britain who are most subject to racist practices tend to be working class, while the definitiion of membership within the ethnic group can often depend on performing gender attributes successfully. Power operates subtly through a complex series of interlocking practices. As a result political challenges to oppressive forms are complex and sometimes contradictory. Sexual politics therefore can never be a single form of activity. They are enmeshed in the whole network of social contradictions and antagonisms that make up the modern world. There is, however, an important point that we can draw from this discussion. Instead of seeing sexuality as a unified whole, we have to recognize that there are various forms of sexuality: there are in fact many sexualities. There are class sexualities, and gender-specific sexualities, there are racial sexualities and there are sexualities of struggle and choice. The 'invention of sexuality' was not a single event, now lost in a distant past. It is a continuing process in which we are simultaneously acted upon and actors, objects of change, and its subjects.

REFERENCES

[1] Carole S. Vance (ed.), *Pleasure and Danger. Exploring Female Sexuality,* Routledge & Kegan Paul, Boston and London (1984), p. 17.

[2] Vern L. Bullough, *Sex, Society and History,* Science History Publications, New York (1976; the particular essay, 'Sex in history: a virgin field', was first published in 1972).

[3] Gordon, Rattray Taylor, *Sex in History,* Thames & Hudson, London (1953), p. 13.

[4] Kenneth Plummer, *Sexual Stigma. An Interactionist Account,* Routledge & Kegan Paul, London (1975), p. 4.

[5] Alfred C. Kinsey, Wardell B. Pomeroy, Clyde E. Martin and Paul H. Gebhard, *Sexual Behavior in the Human Female,* W. B. Saunders Company, Philadelphia and London (1953), p.448.

[6] Richard Dawkins, *The Selfish Gene,* Granada, St Albans (1978), p. x. I discuss sociobiology in Chapter 3 below.

[7] Robert A Padgug, 'Sexual matters: on conceptualizing sexuality in history', *Radical History Review,* No. 20, Spring/Summer 1979: special issue on 'Sexuality in History'.

[8] Rosalind Coward, *Patriarchal Precedents: Sexuality and Social Relations,* Routledge & Kegan Paul, London (1983).

[9] Margaret Mead, *Coming of Age in Samoa. A Study of Adolescence and Sex in Primitive Societies,* Penguin, Harmondsworth (1977; first published 1928). For a highly critical dissection of this work see Derek Freeman, *Margaret Mead and Samoa. The Making and Unmaking of an Anthropological Myth,* Harvard University Press, Cambridge, Mass., and London (1983).

[10] The phrase is used in Bronislaw Malinowski, 'Culture as a determinant of behavior', reprinted in his *Sex, Culture and Myth,* Rupert Hart-Davis, London (1963), p. 167.

[11] J. H. Gagnon and William Simon, *Sexual Conduct. The Social Sources of Human Sexuality,* Hutchinson, London (1973).

[12] Michel Foucault, *The History of Sexuality,* Vol. 1, *An Introduction,* trans. Robert Hurley, Allen Lane, London (1979), p. 105.

[13] Sue Cartledge and Joanna Ryan (eds.), *Sex and Love. New Thoughts on Old Contradictions,* The Women's Press, London (1983), p. 1.

[14] Bronislaw Malinowski, *Sex, Culture and Myth,* Ruper Hart-Davis, London (1963), p. 120, p. 127.

[15] Lawrence Stone, *The Family, Sex and Marriage in England 1500–1800,* Weidenfeld & Nicolson, London (1977), p. 15.

[16] Ellen Ross and Rayna Rapp, 'Sex and society: a research note from social history and anthropology', in Ann Snitow, Christine Stansell and Sharon Thompson (eds.), *Desire: The Politics of Sexuality,* Virago, London (1984), p. 109. The USA edition was published as *Powers of Desire: The Politics of Sexuality,* Monthly Review Press, New York (1983).

[17] Jeremy Cherfas and John Gribbin, *The Redundant Male,* The Bodley Head, London (1984).

[18] Plummer, *Sexual Stigma.*

[19] Compare, for example, J. C. Messenger's account of 'Sex and re-pression in an Irish folk community', in D. S. Marshall and R. C. Suggs, *Human Sexual Behavior: Variations across the Ethnographic Spectrum,* Basic Books, London (1971).

[20] Abdelwahab Bouhdiba, *Sexuality in Islam ,* trans. Alan Sheridan, Routledge & Kegan Paul, London (1985), p. 159, p. 200.

[21] Dennis Altman, *The Homosexualization of America, The Americani-zation of the Homosexual,* St Martin's Press, New York (1982). For a discussion of the impact of AIDS see Chapter 5 below.

[22] C. S. Ford and F. A. Beach, *Patterns of Sexual Behavior,* Methuen, London (1965; first published 1952); Kinsey *et al.,* op cit. Compare comments in Michael Argyle and Monika Henderson, *The Anatomy of Relationships,* Heinemann, London (1985), p. 159.

[23] F. Edholm, 'The unnatural family', in Elizabeth Whitelegg *et al., The Changing Experience of Women,* Martin Robertson, Oxford (1982).

[24] See summary in Ford and Beach, op. cit.

[25] Bronislaw Malinowski, *The Sexual Life of Savages,* Routledge & Kegan Paul, London (1929).

[26] Kenneth Plummer, 'Sexual diversity: a sociological perspective', in K. Howells (ed.), *Sexual Diversity,* Blackwell, Oxford (1984).

[27] Jean Renvoize, *Incest: A Family History,* Routledge & Kegan Paul, London (1982).

[28] Marshall Sahlins, *The Use and Abuse of Biology: An Anthropological Critique of Sociobiology,* Tavistock, London (1976), p. 75.

[29] For fuller details see the discussion in Jeffrey Weeks, *Sex, Politics and*

Society: The Regulation of Sexuality Since 1800, Longman, Harlow (1981), Chapter 4.

[30] See Diana Gittins, *Fair Sex: Family Size and Structure 1900–1939,* Hutchinson, London (1982).

[31] See my *Coming Out. Homosexual Politics in Britain from the 19th Century to the Present,* Quartet, London (1977).

[32] Kinsey *et al., Sexual Behavior in the Human Female,* p. 259.

[33] Angus McLaren, *Reproductive Rituals,* Methuen, London (1984), p. 147. Angus McLaren, *Birth Control in Nineteenth Century England,* Croom Helm, London (1978), p. 390.

[34] See Weeks, *Coming Out.*

[35] Sigmund Freud, 'Three essays on the theory of sexuality', in James Strachey (ed.), *The Standard Edition of the Complete Psychological Works of Sigmund Freud,* Vol. 7, Hogarth Press and The Institute of Psychoanalysis, London (1953–1974).

[36] Paul Veyne, 'Homosexuality in ancient Rome', in Philippe Ariès and André Bejin (eds.), *Western Sexuality: Practice and Precept in Past and Present Times,* Blackwell, Oxford (1985), p. 27.

[37] Jean-Louis Flandrin, 'Sex in married life in the early Middle Ages: the Church's teaching and behavioural reality', in Ariès and Bejin, op. cit., p. 115.

[38] Ibid., p. 126.

[39] See the discussion in Jeffrey Weeks, *Sexuality and its Discontents. Meanings, Myths and Modern Sexualities,* Routledge & Kegan Paul, London (1985), pp. 89–91, and Chapter 8.

[40] Lillian Faderman, *Surpassing the Love of Men,* Junction Books, London (1981).

[41] Alan Bray, *Homosexuality in Renaissance England,* Gay Men's Press, London (1982), p. 114.

[42] Donald M. Lowe, *History of Bourgeois Perception,* Chicago University Press, Chicago (1982), p. 100.

[43] Edwin Schur, *The Politics of Deviance: Stigma Contests and the Uses of Power,* Prentice-Hall, Englewood Cliffs, N.J. (1980), p. 7.

[44] Veyne, op. cit., p. 31.

[45] See for example the arguments of L. Coveney *et al., The Sexuality Papers. Male Sexuality and the Social Control of Women,* Hutchinson, London (1984).

[46] Rosalind Coward, *Female Desire. Women's Sexuality Today,* Paladin, London (1984), p. 13.

[47] Richard Dyer, 'Male sexuality in the media', in Andy Metcalf and Martin Humphries, *The Sexuality of Men,* Pluto Press, London (1985), p. 28.

[48] Carole Vance, *Pleasure and Danger,* p. 4.

[49] See the summary of evidence in Valerie Amos and Pratibha Parmar, 'Challenging imperial feminism', in *Feminist Review* No. 17, 'Black feminist perspectives', July 1984; and Floya Anthias and Nira Yuval-Davis, 'Contextualizing feminism — gender, ethnic and class divisions', *Feminist Review* No. 15, Winter 1983.

3

The meanings of sexual difference

Q. Was your first partner a man or a woman?
A. I was too polite to ask.

(Interview with the novelist Gore Vidal)

THE BIOLOGICAL IMPERATIVE

Gore Vidal's characteristic response to a mildly cheeky question amuses and perhaps jolts us because in our culture whom we have sex with *matters*. Gender, the social condition of being male or female, and sexuality, the cultural way of living out our bodily pleasures and desires, have become inextricably linked, with the result that crossing the boundary between proper masculine or feminine behaviour (that is, what is culturally defined as appropriate) sometimes seems the ultimate transgression. We still cannot think about sexuality without taking into account gender; or, to put it more generally, the elaborate facade of sexuality has in large part been built upon the assumption of fundamental differences between men and women, and of male dominance over women. The genital and reproductive distinctions between biological men and biological women have been read not only as a necessary but also as a sufficient explanation for different sexual needs and desires. They appear as the most basic distinctions between peoples, deeply rooted in our 'animal natures'.

It is one of the peculiarities of us humans that we seek answers to some of our most fundamental questions by looking at the lives of animals. That most despised and feared of all creatures, the rat, has had a high profile in sex research, especially in experimental investigations into the effects of 'male' and 'female' hormones. Many other researchers have found evidence and support for their wildest hypotheses about sexual difference in everthing from insects and the humble worm to the seaside sparrow and rhesus monkeys. In the process, much no doubt has been learnt — especially about animal behaviour. But much remains inexplicable by such methods.

Unfortunately for the simplicities of research, human being are complex, arbitrary and changeable creatures. We manipulate language to constantly reshape our perceptions of the world — and of sex. We defy the apparent logic of our external appearances. We blur the edges between masculinity and femininity. We create differences that transcend the differences of gender (of age, race, sexual need). and we construct boundaries that have little logic 'in Nature'. We even change our behaviour in response to moral, political or accidental factors. Yet all the time we like to indulge the fantasy that our sexuality is the most basic, the most natural, thing about us, and that the relations between men and women are laid down for all eternity, like fingerprints in concrete, by the dictates of our inborn 'nature'. In a culture preoccupied with sexual difference, as ours is, such beliefs have crucial social effects: to repeat, the way we think about sex shapes the way we live it. So discussions about the origins and form of the differences between men and women are much more than obscure debates. They are central to the direction of our society.

John Money has noted 'the cultural practice, taken for granted in our culture, of maximizing the differences, behavioral included, between the sexes, rather than maximizing the similarities' [1]. The 'science of sex' cannot be blamed for this, given the deeply embedded cultural assumptions the early sexologists encountered: in many ways they merely theorized what they believed they saw. Moreover, many of them, alive to empirical reality, were eventually anxious to assert the overlap as much as the differences. For Havelock Ellis in the 1930s, sex was 'mutable', its frontiers uncertain, with 'many stages between a complete male and a complete female' [2]. Yet at the same time the search for the essentially feminine and the essentially masculine continued, with the inevitable result that sexual differences were stressed at the expense of similarities. Sexology became a weapon in the endemic conflict over the appropriate social roles of men and women that accentuated in the last decades of the nineteenth century and has continued, with varying rhythms and intensity, ever since.

The very definition of the sexual instinct was essentially one derived from male practices and fantasies. Just consider some of the metaphors deployed in writings on sex: overpowering forces, engulfing drives, gushing streams, uncontrollable spasms . . . such imagery has dominated the Western discourse on sex. Early sexologists drew on this imagery even as they attempted to put it on a more scientific basis. So sex was defined as a 'physiological law', 'a force generated by powerful ferments', a drive 'which cannot be set aside for any sort of social convention', and most graphically of all, 'a volcano that burns down and lays waste all around it; . . . an abyss that devours all honour, substance and health' [3]. The Darwinian revolution in biology, which demonstrated that man was part of the animal world, encouraged the search for the animal in man, and found it in his sex.

Female sexuality was inevitably a problem — an enigma, a 'dark continent' in Freud's famous words — for such views. A long cultural tradition held that female sexuality was voracious, all-devouring and consuming. This has had a significant recent revival in comments (by men) that modern feminism has exhausted and enfeebled men by encouraging female sexual demands. Such an argument probably tells us more about male fears and fantasies than it does about women, but it has to be noted nonetheless as a fanciful and persistent myth. But since the nineteenth century the more conventional view has been to treat female sexuality as basically reactive, responsive, brought to life only through some sort of 'reproductive instinct', or kissed into kife by the skill of the wooer, the male. Lesbianism has been particularly problematic for theorists of sex precisely because it was an autonomously female sexuality in which men played no part.

The idea that there is a *fundamental* difference between male and female sexual natures has been a powerful one. Even the recent evidence, building on the observational work of Kinsey and Masters and Johnson, that there is a fundamentally *similar* physiological response amongst men and women, has not undermined the belief in basic psychosexual differences elsewhere [4].

The idea that there are differences between peoples is not in itself dangerous. What is peculiar about sexuality is that certain differences have been seen as so fundamental that they become divisions and even antagonisms. At best there is the argument that though men and women may be different they can still be equal. At worst, assumptions about the forceful nature of the male sexual drive have been used to legitimize male domination over women.

We might think that such beliefs have been sufficiently undermined in recent years, especially through the critiques of modern feminism, to have little credence today. But we would be mistaken. Take the views of some recent writers influential on what has become known as the 'New Right' in Britain and North America. Roger Scruton, an English Conservative philosopher, has counterposed what he vividly describes as the 'unbridled ambition of the phallus', eschewing all obligation, to the nature given role of women to 'quieten what is most vagrant'. For George Gilder, a fervent defender of traditional values, it is only the claims of marriage and the family that can channel the man's 'otherwise disruptive male aggression' into social obligation to fend for his wife and offspring [5]. The feminist case against (culturally encoded) male sexual violence is thus transformed into a defence of sexual division *and* traditional morality. For both writers there is a belief in a refractory human nature, threatening disruption unless constrained by moral will and social orthodoxy.

Views such as this find a justification in the 'new synthesis' of sociobiology, through which biological determinism has enjoyed a modest revival. It is important not to exaggerate the influence of this new would-be science, but at the same time it has made an important impact, and not only on the Right. Sociobiology has been deployed even by liberal sources to explain the intractability to change of social institutions, and some aspects of it have also been used to argue for greater freedom for sexual minorities on the grounds of their biological functionality. We need, therefore, to be alive to its appeal — as well as to the dangers I believe to be inherent in it. Sociobiology has been defined by its founding father, E. O. Wilson, as 'the systematic study of the biological basis of all social behavior' [6]. It aims to bridge the gap which had opened up between traditional biological theories on the one hand and social explanations on the other by attempting to demonstrate that there was a key mechanism linking both. This mechanism, in the words of one of Wilson's early enthusiasts, was 'the fundamental law of gene selfishness' [7]. The gene is the basic unit of heredity, defined as a portion of the DNA molecule which affects the development of any trait at the most elementary biochemical level. It carries the code which influences future development. So much may be generally agreed. Where sociobiologists go further is by arguing — going enthusiastically beyond Wilson's initially more tentative positions — that genes exist for every social phenomenon, so that the random survival of the genes could explain all social practices from economic efficiency and educational attainment to gender divisions and sexual preference. In this mode of thought the fundamental unit is no longer 'the individual', as in classical liberal theory; nor is it 'society', as in the great alternative tradition. The individual is now viewed as little more than a vehicle for the transmission of genes, 'a selfish machine, programmed to do whatever is best for his genes as a whole' [8]. If this is true, then the great conflict between individual and society can be simply dissolved: a continuum exists between the timeless energy of the gene, and the most complex social manifestations, with 'society and nature working in harmony'. So what about apparently social institutions like marriage, parenting, social bonding? They were 'adaptive', in the key term of sociobiology, products not of history or social development but of 'evolutionary necessity'. And what about ideas, ideals, values and beliefs? They are, according to Wilson, no more than 'enabling mechanisms for survival' [9].

Given this certainty, the existence of but *two* sexes is paradoxically a problem for sociobiology. Sex, E. O. Wilson argues, is an antisocial force in evolution, for it causes difficulty between people. The male/female relationship is one of mutual mistrust and exploitation. Altruism, necessary for gene survival, is more likely when everyone is the same. So why is human reproduction not carried out through parthenogenesis, as it is with some primitive creatures? And why are there two, not three, four or five sexes? 'To be perfectly honest', Cherfas and Gribbin admit, 'nobody knows' [10]. Which is why, they decide, sex is such an enigma. The most likely reason for sexed reproduction, sociobiologists have ultimately decided after much shuffling of their index cards, is that it promotes diversity, the ability to shuffle the genetic pack to hedge bets against an unpredictably changing environment. Two sexes are just enough to ensure the maximum potential genetic recombination. Two sexes also ensure health and hardiness, by mixing the chemical constituents sufficiently to produce immunity against disease. So men's job 'is to provide the means by which females can fight off disease' [11]: far from being 'redundant', men are still essential for the future of the human race.

Whatever the intricate (and sometimes metaphysical) speculations, one outstanding conclusion flows from all this: 'with respect to sexuality, there is a female human nature and a male human nature, and these natures are extraordinarily different . . .' [12]. These differences begin and end, it appears, with the evolutionary characteristics of the ova and testes. Because males have an almost infinite number of sperm (millions with each ejaculation), while women have a very restricted supply of eggs (around 400 per lifetime), it is deduced that men have an evolutionary propulsion towards spreading their seed to ensure diversity and reproductive success, and hence towards promiscuity, while women have an equal interest in reserving energy, an instinct for conservation, and hence a leaning towards monogamy. From this can be deduced the explanation of all the other supposedly fundamental differences: greater competition between men than between women, a greater male tendency towards polygamy and jealousy whereas women are 'more malleable' and amenable, and a greater sexual will and arousal potential in men than in women:

> Among all peoples copulation is considered to be essentially a service or favor that women render to men, and not vice versa, regardless of which sex desires or is thought to desire greater pleasure from sexual intercourse. [13]

There is a certain intoxicating charm in sociobiology, especially as it offers to end the deadlock in social explanations which the social sciences generally seemed to be encountering by the 1970s. It also — and this is its prize attribute — seems to speak to widespread, commonsense beliefs about the naturalness of sexual divisions. It goes with, rather than against, the grain of popular prejudice. But if it can claim to explain some things (love at first sight 'may simply be the powerful response of the body to the scent of a very different set of histocompatibility antigens'; homosexuality may be necessary to encourage altruistic concern for the offspring of siblings), it cannot generally or convincingly explain others (why there are variations between different cultures, for example, or why history frequently undergoes rapid social change). It is also, as an approach, ultimately deeply conservative in its implications, for if the explanation of what we do, socially and sexually, lies in the haphazard collision of genes, then there is little we can do to change things: bend the twig a little here, unbend it there, but not too much either way in case the whole branch breaks off. If, as H. J. Eysenck and Glenn Wilson reaffirm, there is 'a strong, underlying biological source for the widely differing sexual attitudes we observe when we look at men and women' [14], then feminist demands — or even liberal reforms — are utopian. As some earlier advocates of biological determinism put it, in the context of an earlier upsurge of feminist activity, 'What was decided among the prehistoric protozoa cannot be annulled by Act of Parliament'. There seems little argument about that.

Some or all of this may of course be true. The problem is that while evidence from biology and natural history may be suggestive, it cannot be conclusive. It may be impossible finally to disprove a sociobiological hypothesis — who knows what 'science' will turn up? — it is equally difficult to prove it. In the real world of sexuality in which we live, things are a little more complex than the high priests of the 'sexual tradition' (amongst whom we must now count the sociobiologists) like to think. The most ardent advocates of biological determinism generally display three characteristic modes of argument: argument by analogy; a reliance, amounting almost to an intellectual tyranny, on 'average statements'; and finally what I shall call, for want of a better phrase, the 'black hole' hypothesis. They are all fraught with difficulties.

(1) Argument by analogy

This assumes that by observing animals in the wild we can crack the code of our civilization. A new emphasis on observing animals in their natural habitat during the inter-war years was one of the roots of sociobiology. E. O. Wilson devoted most of his first attempts at a synthesis to insects and birds. The trouble here is that despite all efforts at neutral observation, human prejudices insensibly creep in. As Rose *et al.* have put it:

> Again and again, in order to support their claims to the inevitabi-
> lity of a given feature of the human order, biological determinists
> seek to imply the universality of their claims. If male dominance
> exists in humans, it is because it exists also in baboons, in lions, in
> ducks, or whatever. The ethological literature is replete with
> accounts of 'harem-keeping' by baboons, the male lion's domina-
> tion of 'his' pride, 'gang-rape' in mallard ducks, 'prostitution' in
> humming birds. [15]

It should hardly need saying that what is happening here is the attribution of highly coloured social explanations to animal behaviour. Why should groupings of female animals be seen as harems? They could equally well be seen, for all the counter-evidence available, as prototypes of women's consciousness-raising groups. To say that perhaps evokes a smile. But so should the circular argument by which explanations drawn from human experience are attributed to animals and then used to justify social divisions in the present.

(2)   The tyranny of averages

This is perhaps the most insidious argument of all. *On average,* men may be more sexually active than women. Male homosexuals *may* be more promis-cuous than female homosexuals. This *may,* as sociobiologists argue, have something to do with the genes. It may equally have something to do with culture: greater apportunities for male sexual expression, and for choice of partners, for example. More fundamentally, to say that on average men have more sexual activity than women is tantamount to saying that some women are more sexually active than some men. Average statements are both true and not particularly useful. Yet they carry an enormous weight, in part at least because we prefer clear-cut divisions to ambiguity. Nature herself, however, can be very ambivalent, as the very idea of 'averages' suggests. Why aren't we?

(3)   The 'black hole' hypothesis

This is the final resort for those who can find no other explanation for sexual differences. If all else fails to explain human phenomena, then a biological explanation *must* exist. If more men than women are in top jobs, then biology surely explains it. If society is resistant to the politics of feminism, then it must be because it goes against human nature. If homosexuality can be explained neither by sociology nor psychoanalysis, then biology (hor-mones, instincts, genes . . .) must explain it. There is a classic example of this at the conclusion of the final report of the Kinsey Institute on homosexuality, *Sexual Preferences* [16]. The authors carefully explore the lack of evidence for a single cause of homosexuality, and conclude that there was no evidence for one in sociology or psychology. But instead of then testing the hypothesis (which Kinsey himself had endorsed) that homosexuality was not, therefore, a unitary condition, with single roots, the authors conclude that there must be a biological explanation. This, in the context of the book, is empty speculation. The 'solution' owes more to the continuing prestige of biological sciences than evidence. Biology fills a gap which social explanations have been unwilling, or unable, to fill.

I have no desire to minimize the importance of biology. Biological capacities clearly provide the potentiality out of which so much that is human is shaped, and set the limit for social activities. Copulation, reproduction, nurturance and death are clearly biological in origin and provide the parameters of human existence. Less cosmic biological factors equally have social effects. Genetic differences (amongst men and amongst women, as well as between them) can affect physical appearances, size, strength, longevity, the colour of hair and eyes. Differential production of hormones can affect sexual maturation, distribution of body hair, fat deposition and muscular development. These are not unimportant as they are elaborated in complex cultural codes which lay down the appropriate or inappropriate physical appearance and behaviour of each gender. But it is, ultimately, the social meanings that we give to these differences that is of real importance. If, as John Nicholson has said, 'the biological differences between the sexes are actually minute when compared with the similarities' [17] and in fact, only one gene out of 100,000 needed to make up each person distinguishes men from women, then the critical markers that we conventionally use to demarcate difference need to be re-evaluated.

Anatomical differences are apparently the most basic of all. It is on the presence or absence of the male or female organs that gender is immediately assigned at birth. Yet, the possession of a penis or vagina cannot be a universally applicable standard. In birds, the male does not have a penis; other animals have only 'intromittent organs', such as claspers in sharks and dogfish [18]. Even amongst us humans the meanings of these very real organs are not transparent. The vagina can be conceived of as passive, or as all-devouring. The clitoris has been conceptualized as no more than a 'vestigial phallus', and as the site of women's multi-orgasmic potential. The penis has an even more supercharged symbolic value in our culture. Its 'thrusting', 'forceful', 'penetrative' nature has been seen as the very model of active male sexuality. But, as Richard Dyer has sharply pointed out, there is a marked discrepancy between this symbolism and the way the penis is often experienced:

> Male genitals are fragile, squashy, delicate things . . . penises are
> only little things (even big ones) without much staying power,
> pretty if you can learn to see them like that, but not magical or
> mysterious or powerful in themselves, that is, not objectively full
> of real power. [19]

The significance we give to the male and female organs is important both
socially and psychologically. If we follow the insights of psychoanalysis,
then the existence or absence of the male penis (that is, the fear or fantasy
of castration) is critical for the negotiation of the Oedipal crisis, and for the
acquisition or non-acquisition of psychological masculinity and femininity,
the very organization of sexual difference. But the critical meanings we
assign to them are according to Freud, demanded by culture and do not
arise straightforwardly from the biology alone.

The same potential ambiguity exists over two other, less obvious
markers, the chromosomal make-up of men and women, and hormonal
patterns. The existence, firstly, of chromosomal differences is well known.
The distinction is the one made in international sporting competitions for
defining the sexes, where competitors, in women's athletic events particularly, have to undergo a sex chromosome test [20]. Human beings have in
the nucleus of every cell in their body 46 chromosomes: twenty-two pairs,
and two sex chromosomes. In females these are identical (XX); but in
males one is an incomplete structure, carrying little genetic material (the Y
chromosome: men generally have an XY pairing).

The difficulty is that these are not absolute markers. Sometimes
chromosomes do not separate during cell division in the usual way, giving
rise to XXY, X, XXX, or XYY patterns: are they male or female?
Sometimes there are individuals whose chromosomes say one thing, and
their appearance another: males in that they have XY chromosomes, and
possess testes which secrete the male hormone; but ambiguous in that they
have not, through congenital androgen insensitivity, become externally
masculinized. Even Nature, in her wisdom, apparently makes mistakes.
Abnormalities such as these, Archer and Lloyd conclude [21], 'illustrate
the complex and precarious nature of the development process' — and
hence of the division between the sexes.

Similarly, and secondly, the importance assigned to hormones, the
chemical messengers secreted by the glands, has been exaggerated. The
main hormone produced by the testes is testosterone; this, together with
hormones of the same general type, are called *androgens,* the 'male
hormone'. The main hormones produced by the ovaries are oestrogen and

progesterone (the 'female hormones'). These hormones are undoubtedly important for development: testosterone produces important changes at adolescence, including a deepening voice and the appearance of body hair. The rise of oestrogen levels in girls at puberty encourages breast development, fat redistribution and the beginning of the menstrual cycle. But even so, we are not talking of uniquely male and female possessions. Ovaries and testes each produce all three hormones, and the adrenal glands secrete androgens in both sexes. What differs is the ratio. Again there is no absolute divide. As Kinsey put it some time ago:

> The fact that hormones are produced in the gonads is, without further evidence, no reason for believing that they are the primary agents controlling those capacities of the nervous system on which sexual response depends. [22]

Hormones, no more than chromosomes, are decisive in shaping social and psychic sexual differences.

SEXUALITY AND SOCIAL RELATIONS

Biological determinism insists on the fixity of our sexualities, on their resilience in the face of all efforts at modification. Social and historical explanations, on the other hand, assume a high degree of fluidity and flexibility in 'human nature', in its potentiality for change. The evidence of other cultures, and of different periods of our own, show that there are many different ways of being 'men' and 'women', alternative ways of living social life. The experience of our own recent past has shown the powerful ways in which an energetic social movement — of feminism — with little institutional support can influence and in many cases transform sexual relations. Imagine the power of rapid social change in the past. Our growing awareness of other cultures should make us more attentive to alternative forms of interaction — not least because through the perspective of cultural difference and change we can begin to reflect on the historical contingency of our own 'human nature', and question the supposed fixity of our own positions as 'men' and 'women'.

The overwhelming evidence suggests that sexuality is subject to an enormous degree of socio-cultural moulding, to the extent that, as Plummer has suggested, 'sexuality has no meaning other than that given to it in social situations' [23]. But to put it like this does not, of course, resolve difficulties; it merely pushes them along a rather different path. For if sex and sexual difference are social in form, we still need to know where we can set the limits of purely social explanations, what the boundaries against cultural moulding are. Is sex entirely a matter of social naming? Is there a complete interchangeability of roles between men and women? Are our sexual natures infinitely plastic, 'unbelievably malleable' in the famous words of Margaret Mead? Such questions inevitably come to mind, and it must be admitted that we are still quite unsure of the appropriate answers. We know what our sexual natures are not: they are not eternally fixed, biologically determined, and unchangeable. We are not so certain what they are.

There is a real danger therefore of confronting an inadequate biological essentialism with an equally inadequate sociological essentialism, in which the malleability of sexuality is always at the bidding of deterministic social imperatives. For the enormously influential social anthropologists of the inter-war years it was not human nature but the 'cultural configuration' that was the main object of concern. This was a real gain in that it forced a rethink of many cherished sociological 'truths'. But there were, nevertheless, real problems with the cultural relativism that emerged. Each culture presented itself as a necessary and inexplicable set of differences from others. History, development and change were not issues high on the agenda. Each society, moreover, was seen as imposing itself on its inhabitants as a totality in which all social positions were *necessary* responses to societal demands. This type of argument has been taken up by many later writers to argue for the functionality of sex roles. Individuals 'accept and reproduce', Weinstein and Platt have written, 'the patterns of behavior required by society', with the family as the main conduit for this social moulding, and neatly complementary 'social roles' as the necessary result [24]. There does not seem to be much room for manoeuvre in this. Not only is society seen as the prime mover, but individuals, we must presume, are blank sheets, *tabula rasa,* on which are imprinted the required characteristics needed to make that society function adequately. Society organizes a sexual division of labour to fulfil its demands — in reproduction, nurturance, employment, household activities, and sex. It even creates deviant and stigmatized social roles — for example, the 'role' of homosexuals in our culture — both to provide slots for those who cannot quite fit in, and to act as a warning to the rest of society of the awesome effects of stepping out of line.

Such arguments obviously have an appeal. They offer an elegant explanation for the obvious differences and divisions we see around us. But there is a problem with any theory which endows 'society' with a conscious will, and which believes that all the parts fit together like a marvellous clockwork: where do people and their subjective wills come in? Moreover, there is a curiously paradoxical result of this stress on social moulding. In emphasizing the social as the prime mover, certain characteristics of 'nature' are not questioned. More specifically, in most socially deterministic accounts the necessity for a sexual division of labour along lines of anatomical differences is not challenged but reaffirmed.

This is clear in the work of Margaret Mead, who battled harder than most to suggest the flexibility of human nature. In *Sex and Temperament in Three Primitive Societies* she found a great range of sex variations in New Guinea [25]. The Arapesh had no strong idea of sex as an overpowering force in either men or women, and both sexes had qualities that could be called 'maternal'. Amongst the Mundugumor, on the other hand, both men and women were positively sexed and aggressive. In the third tribe, the Tchambuli, there was a full reversal of the sex attitudes of our own culture, with women as dominant and men emotionally dependent. In a later work, summarizing the evidence, Mead suggested that 'In every known society, mankind has elaborated the biological division of labour into forms often very remotely related to the original biological differences that provided the original clues . . . sometimes one quality has been assigned to one sex, sometimes to the other' [26]. Yet, at the same time as the possibility of social moulding is reaffirmed, those 'original clues' assume a critical importance. For if human society is to survive, she argues, 'it must have a pattern of social life that comes to terms with the differences between the sexes' [27]. What are these? Reproductive capacities are clearly different between men and women, and even the development of reproductive technologies are unlikely to change this fundamentally. On the basis of these differences, cultures have elaborated separated roles — for parenting, nurturance, work and household organization. But as Mead's own writings show, the form of those roles vary enormously, with men and women interchangeable in the qualities we describe as 'maternal' and 'paternal'. If social roles are so flexible, if there is no necessary connection between reproduction, gender and sexual attributes, it is not clear why sharp sexual dichotomies should be so crucially necessary — unless we make a prior assumption about their inevitability. It is difficult to avoid the conclusion that in the end Mead takes for granted the prime significance of anatomy: anatomical difference guarantees the roles required by society. This may be true, but why this should be so is never questioned. Surely it is of prime importance to know why so many cultures have chosen anatomy as the fundamental basis of our social destinies.

We need to go beyond the simplicities of some of these explanations. I want to suggest particularly that 'society' is neither as unified and total in its impact as these theories suggest, nor are the lines of difference so clear-cut and decisive. If we look at what we mean by 'society' we find that in practice all social theory confirms the complexity of social relationships, the 'multiple realities' through which we negotiate our everyday lives. 'Society' is not a whole governed by a coherent set of determinants, but an intricate web of institutions, beliefs, habits, ideologies and social practices that have no *a priori* unity and whose actual relationships have to be unravelled rather than taken as read. If we transfer this view of 'the social' to sexual activities, we will see that far from 'society' moulding 'sexuality', in any straightforward way, what we describe as sexual is constructed through a complexity of social relations, each of which has a different view of what constitutes sex and appropriate sexual behaviour. The modern apparatus of sexuality, Michel Foucault has suggested, is heterogeneous, including: 'discourses, institutions, architectural arrangements, regulations, laws, administrative measures, scientific statements, philosophic propositions, morality, philantropy, etc.' [28]. All of these together make up what we define as sexuality, but they clearly do not and cannot all say the same things, or address us in identical ways.

There exists in the world of sexuality a variety of different and often contradictory accounts of what it is to be sexual: organized sets of meanings ('discourses'), articulated through a variety of different languages, and anchored in a dense network of social activities. Traditional Christian concepts of sexual behaviour, for example, rely on certain assumptions about human nature — that it is unregenerate or corrupt, that the division of the sexes was preordained, that sexual activity is only justified by reproduction or love. These beliefs are laid down in a set of statements — biblical interpretations, commentaries, canon law, sermons. They are generalized through a language of certitude and morality, which divides the sinners from the saved, the moral from the immoral. These meanings are embodied in institutions which work to reinforce beliefs and behaviours: churches, the privileged position of parenthood, the practices of confession or testimony before God, the existence of religious schools, the sacraments of baptism and marriage, even, in many countries, the legal system. The totality of these discourses and practices construct 'subject positions', in which the moral elite can recognize themselves as truly among the chosen, and the sinful as beyond the hope of redemption. Individuals are shaped, and shape themselves, in relationship to such pre-existing sets of meaning, which seek to regulate and control their behaviour according to firm and consciously and unconsciously imbibed rules.

It is here that the idea of the 'script', used by some interactionist sociologists to account for the way we take our sexual meanings, provides a powerful, if inevitably ambiguous, metaphor: 'Scripts specify, like blueprints', John Gagnon has suggested, 'the whos, whats, whens, wheres and whys for given types of activity . . . It is like a blueprint or roadmap or recipe, giving directions . . .' [29]. We do not, of course, follow absolutely these guidelines, or we would all be the same, and 'immorality', deviance or transgression would scarcely exist. But the 'scripts' laid down in certain social practices set the parameters within which individual choices are available. There is another value to the metaphor: it suggests that there are a variety of possible sexual meanings coexisting at any one time. In the Christian West we have been subjected to a host of conflicting and often contradictory definitions. Medicine since the nineteenth century has worked hard to displace religion as the major force in the regulation of sexuality. Its language speaks less of morality and more of the 'natural' and 'unnatural', healthy and sick sexualities; its institutional focus is the clinic, hospital or psychiatrist's couch (Michel Foucault was not the first to suggest an analogy between the confessional mode and the talking cure of psychoanalysis: Freud himself made the same connection). Then there are the languages of law, education, anthropology, sociology and politics, all of which speak in carefully differentiated tones about sexuality: is it a product of criminality, nurture, cultural variation, political choice? And of course there are the counter-discourses, the reverse and often militant languages, of the new sexual movements. We live in a world of rival and often contradictory descriptions and definitions.

The emergence of clear-cut sexual differences is therefore a prolonged process for each individual subject, learned in all the complexities of social life. Family life provides models, though these are by no means clear-cut. Schools convey clear messages, though not always in the same direction. Peer group assessment guards the barricades against social deviance. Rituals of courtship, sexual initiation, even sexual violence affirm divisions. Desires and choices of partner secure the path of normality or the road to unorthodox behaviour. Media representations construct the images of desirable identities. Religious and moral and political involvements help organize adult ways of life. Even chance brings its wayward influence. It is in response to all these influences — and many more — that we construct our subjectivities, our sense of who we are, how we came to where we are, where we want to go: our identities as men and women, heterosexual and homosexual, or whatever, are a product of complex processes of definition and self-definition in a complex arrangement of social relations.

On the surface, at least, this suggests that male and female identities, far from being fixed for all eternity by natural attributes, are rather fragile and haphazard, subject to a variety of influences and often torn by contradictions. For instance, we learn early on in our particular society that to be a 'man' is to be *not* a homosexual. Male homosexuality has been stigmatized through several centuries as effeminate, an inversion of gender, precisely 'unmanly'. Yet we also know that many 'real men' do see themselves as homosexual, and that the 1970s saw a general 'machoization' of the gay world. Here conventional views about what it is to be a man conflict with sexual desires and (probably) sexual activities: yet for many gay men the two are held in tension. The sexuality of women provides another example: women have been traditionally defined as having a sexuality which is responsive, nurturant and closely associated with reproduction. But over the past few decades, women's bodies have been increasingly sexualized in the media and through representations generally. The same woman can be addressed in the pages of a glossy magazine both as an efficient home-maker, caring and domestic, and as a *femme fatale,* sexual and alluring, with no sense that the different definitions may be in conflict or may have confusing effects. We hold together in our minds and in our sexual make-ups a host of changing, and often warring accounts of ourselves, our motives, our wishes and desires, and our needs.

But the social world does demand distinctions, and creates boundaries. 'Masculinity' and 'femininity' may not be unified concepts. They are fraught with conflicting and contradictory messages, and they have differ-ent meanings in different contexts. They do not mean the same thing in formal social documents or legal codes as they do in popular prejudice. They mean different things in different class, geographical and racial milieux. And yet, whatever the qualifications we make, they exist not only as powerful ideas but as critical social divides. We do it in different ways at different times but we all the time divide people into 'men' and 'women'. More than this, we are not speaking of simple, meaningless differences: we are in fact referring to power differentials and to historical situations where socially and practically men have had the power to define women. Maleness and male sexuality remain the norms by which we judge women. This does not mean that male definitions are simply accepted; on the contrary, there are constant battles over sexual meanings at individual and collective levels. But the battles are against, and within the limits set, by the dominant terms. These in turn are encoded via a social privileging of particular relationships — in marriage and family arrangements and a host of other social institutions and activities, through which gender, and sexual, identi-ties are constructed and constantly reaffirmed.

Perhaps most of this takes place on a level where its subtleties escape our conscious notice. But even amongst young people, as some recent researchers have clearly shown, its weight can be determining. Mica Nava's observations in youth centres suggest the extreme pressures to conform to accepted sexual divisions and heterosexual arrangements that exist and are constantly reinforced amongst adolescents through language, ritual and interaction. In such centres, she writes:

the regulation of girls is enforced largely by *boys* through reference to a notion of femininity which incorporates particular modes of sexual behaviour, deference and compliance . . . In this culture outside the home, girls are observers of boys' activity and *guardians* of girls' passivity . . . Such power is located in groups of boys (and girls) who, through reference to certain discourses and categories — like 'slag' and 'poof' — are able to ensure 'appropriate' masculine and feminine behaviour. [30]

This is a paradigm of how differences are institutionalized and reinforced throughout social life — from work practices ('sexual harassment') to street conventions ('wolf whistles') to routine rituals in bars and other social activities. Despite all the changes that have taken place (Nava's researches took place after a decade of apparently unprecedented publicity given to alternative ways of being men and women) male sexuality as culturally defined provides the norm and, not surprisingly, female sexuality continues to be the problem. Males, in *becoming* men, take up positions in power relations in which they acquire the ability to define women.

SEXUALITY AND THE UNCONSCIOUS

Two major points should stand out from the discussion so far. First, we need to recognize, more readily than we are inclined to do, that sexual identities are not pregiven, automatic or fixed. They are on the contrary socially organized, contingent and changeable. They are also relational. Masculinity and femininity each exist only because of the existence of the other. They are shifting and changing definitions, locked together in an apparently inevitable but all the time changing dance of life and death. Secondly, we seem unable to escape our strong investment in sexual difference, a difference where women are perennially subordinate to men. In part, no doubt, this historical continuity can be explained by reference to the considerable power it does give to men. Advocates of the existence across all cultures of structures of patriarchal power would see this as a sufficient explanation. It cannot explain, however, both the deep commitment we seem to have to sexual difference, nor the strain that is evident in many people's lives, men and women, as they strive to maintain it. Sexual difference is apparently necessary *and* precarious, fundamental yet provisional. How then do we recognize ourselves in these social categories? Why do we invest so much in what appears to modern sexual theory so ephemeral? Why are sexual differences apparently so inessential yet so permanent and resilient? It is at this point that insights can be gained from another theoretical approach, that of psychoanalysis, the theory of the dynamic unconscious and of desire.

Psychoanalysis has made a critical contribution to the theorization of sex during this century, though its impact has often been ambiguous and contradictory. Like so many other of the great intellectual preoccupations of the twentieth century (marxism, democracy and nationalism spring to mind), it has different meanings in different contexts. Freud's own work provides a treasure chest for varying interpretations, while the work of the many who claim to be his legitimate successors takes us down many highways and byways, often to a destination that bears little relationship to what Freud said, or meant, or wanted to believe. It is therefore hazardous in the extreme to venture to describe a 'true Freud'. A more interesting and adventurous route is to look at the way in which recent reinterpretations of Freud have offered a challenge to the orthodoxies of the sexual tradition. Here the critical contribution has come from feminist appropriations of psychoanalysis, drawing largely on the work of the French analyst, Jacques Lacan, and on the investigations of infancy of Melanie Klein, but developing a synthesis which is largely political rather than 'scientific' in its purpose.

Rosalind Coward argues that the importance of psychoanalysis lies in the fact that it precisely did not assume sexuality as an unproblematic category [31]. Rather, psychoanalysis proposed a radical re-examination of the concept of sexuality, questioning the centrality of sexual reproduction and the rigid distinctions between men and women. For her, then, the significance of this approach is that it challenges essentialist views, and problematizes the pre-given nature of sexual difference, at the same time as it recognizes the power of unconscious meanings. This is an important extension and development of Freud's own work. Freud was in fact very clear on the problematic nature of concepts of masculinity and femininity, believing them to be amongst the most difficult known to science. Following from these early Freudian insights, there are three crucial strands in the contemporary appropriation of psychoanalysis. First, there is the theory of the unconscious itself, the very core of psychoanalysis. The psychoanalytic tradition proposes that individuals are not predetermined products of biological imperatives, nor are they the effects simply of social relations. There is a psychic realm — the unconscious — with its own dynamic, rules and history, where the biological possibilities of the body acquire meaning. Chodorow has put this clearly:

> We live an embodied life; we live with those genital and repro-
> ductive organs and capacities, those hormones and chromosomes,
> that locate us physiologically as male and female. But . . . there is
> nothing self-evident about this biology. How anyone under-
> stands, fantasizes about, symbolizes, internally represents, or

feels about her or his physiology is a product of development and experience in the family and not a direct product of the biology itself. [32]

The unconscious is a sphere of conflict: between ideas, wishes, and desires — above all sexual desires — denied access to conscious life by the force of mental repression, yet 'returning' all the time to disrupt consciousness in the form of dreams, slips of the tongue, jokes, neurotic symptoms or perverse behaviour. What fundamentally constitutes the unconscious are those wishes and desires which are repressed in the face of the demands of reality, and in particular the repressed, incestuous desires of infancy: 'What is unconscious in mental life is also what is infantile' [33].

This leads to the second point: to a theorization of sexual difference. Identities — as men and women — and the organization of desires and object choices — as heterosexual, homosexual, or whatever — are not laid down automatically at birth. They are a product of psychic struggle and conflict as the initial 'blob of humanity', with its undifferentiated, polymorphously perverse sexuality, and bisexual nature (object-choice is not pregiven), negotiates the hazard-strewn path to a precarious maturity. The child negotiates the phases of initial development where different parts of the body become focuses of erotic excitement (the oral, anal, phallic and genital phases), advancing through the dawning recognition of 'castration' (the presence or absence of the male organ) to the drama of the Oedipus crisis, in which the young person struggles with incestuous desires for the mother and the father, to an eventual identification with the 'appropriate parent' of the same sex. Through this 'epic' struggle the undifferentiated infant finally becomes a little man or a little woman. This is of course a schematic description which does little justice to the subtle intricacies of Freud's final accounts. There is no inevitable progress to the altar of proper behaviour. If the process 'worked' automatically there would be no ambiguity about gender, no homosexuality, fetishism, transvestism, and so on. I offer the description to underline the point that for Freud attaining sexual identity, and the soldering together of identity and desire (who we are, and what we need and lack), is a struggle that we all have to enter and that by no means ends in a victorious capture of the position allotted to us by reason of our anatomy.

On the other hand, as Freud notoriously wrote, 'Anatomy is destiny' [34], and this is the core of the objections to Freud's theories from the first and ever since. The phrase appears to underpin the intractability of our social arrangements, to justify sexual division, to impose a tyranny of the body over the mind. There is, however, an alternative way of seeing the importance of anatomy: as symbolically important, representative of sexual differences which acquires meaning only in culture. In recent psychoanalytic writings, the penis, or rather its symbolic representative, the phallus, is seen as the prime marker in relation to which meaning is shaped. It is the mark of difference, representing power differences existing in the 'symbolic order', the realm of language, meaning and culture, and of history (and therefore, potentially, of change) [35]. If this is any way an accurate account, then what the child acquires in its access to the order of meaning at the Oedipal moment is a growing awareness of the *cultural* importance of the male organ for subsequent sexual difference and social position. Thus the threat of castration to the boy (if you don't behave I'll cut your thing off . . .) or the culturally produced belief in a 'castration' that has already taken place for the girl (who does not possess a 'thing') become of decisive *psychic* significance. The terror of castration propels the young boy and young girl *differently* through the crisis. Both have to break with the primal connection with their mother, but they break with it differently; the boy through an identification with his father and eventual transference of his love for his mother into a desire for other women (this is what a man is, and does); the girl in a much more difficult and long-drawn process to confirm her identification with the mother and transform her desire to have a penis into a desire to receive the favour of the penis from another (that is, to be a woman receptive to a man).

What matters in this is not so much the detail — which in its crude outline can occasionally seem risible — as the attempt it reveals to show how sexed identities are shaped in a complex human process through which anatomical differences acquire meaning in unconscious life. Our destinies are shaped not so much by the differences themselves but by their meaning, which is socially given and psychically elaborated. But a third point emerges from this: that identities are not only precarious acquisitions, they are provisional ones, 'imaginary closures', which are subject to disruptions all the time, through the eruption of unconscious elements, repressed desires not fully or finally extinguished by the Oedipal drama. For Freud, to be human was to be divided, to be constantly 'decentred', swayed by forces outside conscious control. And at the heart of this fractured subjectivity are the ambiguous meanings of masculinity and femininity:

> For psychology, the contrast between the sexes fades away into one between activity and passivity, in which we far too readily identify activity with maleness and passivity with femaleness, a view which is by no means universally confirmed in the animal kingdom. [36]

At this point Freud can clearly be seen as a precursor of those contemporary accounts which seek to question the fixity of our human nature, and the rigidity of sexual divisions.

THE CONSEQUENCES OF DIFFERENCE

We now have two terms with which to challenge the rigidities of biological determinism: 'the social', a web of institutions, relationships and beliefs, and 'the unconscious', which in many ways mediates between social imperatives and biological possibilities, while having a history of its own. Our sexual identities — as men or women, normal or abnormal, heterosexual or homosexual — are constructed from the diverse materials we negotiate in our life courses, limited by our biological inheritance, altered by contingency, social regulation and control, and subject to constant disruptions from unconscious wishes and desires. Yet at the same time we do not seem able to escape the differences between the sexes. As Denise Riley observes:

> There is a truth in Freud's 'anatomy is destiny' which is unshakeable. Anatomy, *given everything as it is,* points us irresistibly along certain paths, to certain choices. [37]

The pre-existing structures of sexual difference, the subject positions they prescribe and describe necessarily limit the free play of desire *and* the pursuit of other differences, other ways of being human. We are locked into positions whose uncertainties we can acknowledge but whose compelling attractions we seem unable to avoid.

This poses major problems for a feminist or radical sexual politics. If the differences are simply seen as arbitrary and contingent, to be lived through as if they did not really exist, then we dismantle the *raison d'être* of a feminist politics committed to change: that there are historical grounds for the organization of women around their subordination. Feminism then would become no more than a collection of ad hoc policies for the amelioration of gender inequalities. On the other hand, if difference is celebrated in order to affirm the community of all women, as a form of radical feminism would assert, then it is difficult to escape the conclusion that the enemy are men and that division and antagonism are unavoidable.

The question of male sexual violence against women raises these dilemmas acutely. Such violence is endemic, enacted in a series of sexualized situations from rape to domestic violence and child abuse. If we reject, as I believe we should, the belief that this violence is the inevitable byproduct of an inherently aggressive masculinity, and recognize it instead, in Rosalind Coward's words, as 'the ritualistic enactment of cultural meaning about sex' [38] then we must find the explanation in the social and psychic conditions in which masculinity is acquired. These are multiple and complex, and not susceptible to simple resolutions. Sex, as we have seen, is a vehicle for a variety of feelings and needs. But for men, Eardley has argued:

> it becomes heavily charged because of the emotional illiteracy which is part and parcel of male socialisation. So often sex then becomes a bottleneck of pent-up and misdirected yearnings, frustrations and anger . . . The pressure of this mass of undigested and unexperienced emotion which clusters around sexuality is perhaps what gives the myth of male urgency its subjective power for men. [39]

Such an explanation is no doubt partial and inadequate, but it is useful for indicating the blend of factors that do indeed lie at the heart of male aggressiveness, ranging from psychic repression and the conditions of family life to social expectations concerning male behaviour.

But if this is agreed, and male sexual violence is not at all a product of an unproblematic biology but of complex social practices and psychic structuring, the change to transform the relations between men and women can only be brought about by equally complex processes, ranging from new methods of child-rearing to radically different economic, legal and social conditions for women. This has led Riley to the conclusion that

> 'sexual politics' are, despite this exciting coupling of 'sexual' and 'politics', less likely to be productive of the truly revolutionary than the more pedestrian-sounding areas of social and family policies. [40]

What is ultimately involved in this position is not so much an abandonment of a politics around questions of gender and sexuality but rather a recognition of the need to think through appropriate policies and to develop values which go beyond the existing confines of difference.

All of this would suggest that sexual difference as we know it is neither inevitable nor unchangeable. But the precondition for change is a recognition of the interlocking of elements that give it life and allow it to survive. Only with such a perception, I suggest, will it be possible to escape the 'biological imperative' and to explore the range of other differences that provide the potential richness and variety of human (as opposed to animal) life.

REFERENCES

[1] John Money, *Love and Love Sickness,* Johns Hopkins University Press, Baltimore and London (1980), p. 133.

[2] Havelock Ellis, *The Psychology of Sex,* William Heinemann, London (1946; first published 1933), p. 194.

[3] See the discussion in Weeks, *Sexuality and its Discontents. Meanings, Myths and Modern Sexualities,* Routledge & Kegan Paul, London (1985), pp. 80–85.

[4] See William H. Masters and Virginia E. Johnson, *Human Sexual Response,* Little, Brown and Co., Boston (1966).

[5] Roger Scruton, 'The case against feminism', *The Observer,* 22 May, 1983; George F. Gilder, *Sexual Suicide,* Quadrangle, New York (1973).

[6] E. O. Wilson, *Sociobiology: The New Synthesis,* Harvard University Press, Cambridge, Mass., and London (1975), p. 4.

[7] Richard Dawkins, *The Selfish Gene,* Granada, St Albans (1978), p. 7.

[8] Ibid., p. 71.

[9] E. O. Wilson, *On Human Nature,* Harvard University Press, Cambridge, Mass. (1978), p. 3.

[10] Jeremy Cherfas and John Gribbin, *The Redundant Male,* The Bodley Head, London (1984), p. 4.

[11] Ibid., p. 178.

[12] Donald Symons, *The Evolution of Human Sexuality,* Oxford University Press, Oxford and New York (1979), p. 11.

[13] Ibid., pp. 27–28.

[14] H. J. Eysenck and G. D. Wilson, *The Psychology of Sex,* Dent, London (1979), p. 9.

[15] Steven Rose, Leon J. Kamin and R. C. Lewontin, *Not in our Genes. Biology, Ideology and Human Nature,* Penguin, Harmondsworth (1984), p. 158.

[16] Alan P. Bell, Martin S. Weinberg and Sue Kiefer Hammersmith,

Sexual Preference. Its Development in Men and Women, Indiana University Press, Bloomington (1981), pp. 191–192.

[17] John Nicholson, *Men and Women. How Different Are They?* Oxford University Press, Oxford and New York (1984), p. 6.

[18] John Archer and Barbara Lloyd, *Sex and Gender,* Penguin, Harmondsworth (1982), pp. 47–48.

[19] Richard Dyer, in Andy Metcalf and Martin Humphries, *The Sexuality of Men,* Pluto Press, London (1985), pp. 30–31.

[20] Archer and Lloyd, op. cit., p. 47.

[21] Ibid., p. 69.

[22] Alfred C. Kinsey, Wardell P. Pomeroy, Clyde E. Martin and Paul H. Gebhard, *Sexual Behavior in the Human Female,* W. B. Saunders Company, Philadelphia and London (1953), pp. 728–729.

[23] Kenneth Plummer, *Sexual Stigma. An Interactionist Account,* Routledge & Kegan Paul, London (1975), p. 32.

[24] Fred Weinstein and Gerald M. Platt, *The Wish to be Free. Psyche and Value Change,* University of California Press, Berkeley (1969), p. 6.

[25] Margaret Mead, *Sex and Temperament in Three Primitive Societies,* Routledge & Kegan Paul, London (1948), pp. 279–280.

[26] Margaret Mead, *Male and Female. A Study of the Sexes in a Changing World,* Victor Gollancz, London (1949), p. 7.

[27] Ibid., p. 163.

[28] Michel Foucault, *Power/Knowledge,* edited by Colin Gordon, Harvester Press, Brighton (1980), p. 194.

[29] John H. Gagnon, *Human Sexualities,* Scott, Foresman and Co., Glenview, Illinois (1977), p. 6.

[30] Mica Nava, 'Youth service provision, social order and the question of girls', in Angela McRobbie and Mica Nava (eds.), *Gender and Generation,* Macmillan, Basingstoke (1984), pp. 12–13.

[31] Rosalind Coward, *Patriarchal Precedents. Sexuality and Social Relations,* Routledge & Kegan Paul, London (1983).

[32] Nancy Chodorow, 'Gender, relation and difference in psychoanalytic perspective', in Hester Eisenstein and Alice Jardine (eds.), *The Future of Difference,* G. K. Hall, Boston, Mass. (1980), p. 18.

[33] Sigmund Freud, *Introductory Lectures on Psychoanalysis* (1916–17) in *Standard Edition,* Vol. 16, Lecture 13, p. 210. For a fuller discussion of Freud's various theorizations of sexuality, see Weeks, *Sexuality and its Discontents,* Chapter 6.

[34] *Standard Edition,* Vol. 19, p. 178.

[35] See particularly Juliet Mitchell, *Psychoanalysis and Feminism,* Allen Lane, London (1974).

[36] Sigmund Freud, *Civilisation and its Discontents* (1930), *Standard Edition,* Vol. 21, p. 106, note 3.

[37] Denise Riley, *War in the Nursery. Theories of the Child and Mother,* Virago, London (1983), p. 4.

[38] Rosalind Coward, *Female Desire. Women's Sexuality Today,* Paladin, London (1984), p. 239.

[39] Tony Eardley, 'Violence and sexuality' in Metcalf and Humphries, *The Sexuality of Men,* p. 101.

[40] Riley, op. cit.

4

The Challenge of Diversity

Sexualities keep marching out of the *Diagnostic and Statistical Manual* and on to the pages of social.

Gayle Rubin [1]

THE LANGUAGE OF PERVERSITY

If the way we think about sex shapes the way we experience it, then words are tiny marks of those thoughts, haphazard signs scribbled on the page or floating in the air, which we charge with meaning. Let us take two words that are common in discussions about sexuality. The first is 'perversity', the state of being 'perverse' or 'perverted', a turning away from what is proper and right. The second is 'diversity', the condition of being 'diverse', concerning 'difference' or 'unlikeness'. The two words are clearly related, each of them suggesting a move away from a strict 'normality' (another key word). *The Shorter Oxford English Dictionary* acknowledges the link by recording as one meaning of 'diversity' the word 'perversity', a usage it dates back to the sixteenth century. There is clearly a common history. Yet when applied to sexuality, the implications of these words today are distinct. Perversity and diversity may appear to refer to the same phenomenon. In reality a chasm has opened between them signifying a major shift in the language of sexuality and the way we think about our needs and desires. For while all the terms relating to 'perversity' suggest a hierarchy of sexual values in which 'the perversions' are right at the bottom of the scale, 'diversity' hints at a continuum of behaviours in which one element has no more fundamental a value than any other.

The language of the perverse has always had a strongly moral accent, implying a turning away from what is right, an indulgence in wrong. It is laden with opprobrium. The utilization of terms like perversion and pervert in the sexological writings of the late nineteenth century therefore carried a powerful charge. These terms arose, according to Havelock Ellis (who had himself had shown no small skill in deploying them in his earlier writings), at a time when 'sexual anomalies were universally regarded as sins or crimes, at the least as vices' [2]. As a result prohibitions which were rooted in ancient Christian codes were transferred, willy-nilly, to the ostensibly scientific language of the sexological textbooks. Here they became the framework in which clinical investigation of individual sexual lives were conducted, providing definitions, Kinsey sharply commented, nearly identical with 'theologic classifications and with moral pronouncements of the English common law of the fifteenth century' [3]. Homosexuality, fetishism, voyeurism, kleptomania, sadism and masochism, transvestism, coprophilia, undinism, frottage, chronic satyriasis and nymphomania, necrophilia, pederasty . . . the list was endless. Each perversion was investigated with dispassionate care and its causes were endlessly speculated upon. Was it a degeneration or a harmless anomaly, congenital or acquired, the result of tainted heredity or the effects of moral corruption, a product of psychic trauma or free and wilful choice? Krafft-Ebing offered a distinction between a *perversion* and a *perversity,* the latter a product of vice, the former a psycho-pathological condition. Havelock Ellis distinguishes between *inversion,* a more or less random biological 'sport', and *perversion,* which sprang from moral indulgence. Magnus Hirschfeld and his followers distinguished *perversions* from *anomalies.* But whatever the speculations about precise demarcations or aetiologies (causes), there was no doubt about the result. Walking out of the pages of these sexological writings, speaking in authentic tones of self-confession (even if their more outrageous memories were carefully censored, accompanied by lines of dots, or rendered in Latin) were real individual beings, marked or marred by their badges of sexual unorthodoxy.

The result of what Foucault has described as the 'perverse implantation' [4] was twofold. On the positive side, the description of these new types of sexual being considerably expanded the definition of what could be considered as 'sexual'. Freud opened his *Three Essays on the Theory of Sexuality* in 1905 with a discussion of homosexuality and other 'sexual aberrations' precisely because he believed that their existence transformed conventional views as to what constituted sex. He used them, as Laplanche and Pontalis put it, 'as a weapon with which to throw the traditional definitions of sexuality into question' [5]. The new definition extended backwards to include even the most modest whispers of infantile sexuality (attachment to the breast, contraction of the bowels, manipulation of the genitals, a generalized sensuality, as well as less overt but more significant Oedipal anxieties) and outwards to the farthest reaches of human behaviour, to embrace not only common or garden variations but also esoteric manifestations that had little obvious connection with orgasm or even pleasure at all. Here were the seeds of a modern view of an infinite sexual variety. But the negative side of this classificatory enthusiasm was a sharp reinforcement of 'the normal'. There was little discussion of heterosexuality as such (there still isn't). The term itself emerged, almost reluctantly, *after* homosexuality and originally referred to what we now call bisexuality. Even today it has a vaguely clinical tone to it which limits its common use in everyday speech. But the very absence of speculation about its fundamental nature reinforced its taken-for-granted status. Moreover, the debates over the causes of the perversions and the eager descriptions of even their most outrageous examples inevitably worked to emphasize their pathology, their relationship to degeneracy, madness and sickness, and helped to reinforce the normality of heterosexual relations. This served to reinvigorate that disease model of sexuality which has enormously influenced twentieth-century ways of thinking about sexual behaviour.

Take, for instance, Freud's attempt to argue for the broadening of the meaning of sexuality. Perversions, he argued, are simply acts which either *extend* sexual practices beyond those regions of the body conventional designated as appropriate (that is the genitals of either sex), or *linger* over activities that may be proper if they ultimately lead to genital sexuality (the so-called forepleasure, such as kissing, caressing, sucking, biting), but which become perverse if they remain as ends in themselves [6]. This may be a fair working definitions and it is more generous in its inclusiveness than many others on offer. It is, however, difficult to avoid the conclusion that there is in his mind a model of what sex should be, a goal towards which sexual practices ought to be directed, and hence a prescription of how we must live.

Freud was an interesting example of the ambivalence of these early scientists of sex for the very reason that the he went further than anyone else in incorporating the perverse within the acceptable range of sexuality. The effect of *The Three Essays* was to suggest that perversions, far from being the unique property of a sick or immoral minority are the common property of us all. Their negative was revealed in neurotic symptoms, which were displaced representations of repressed sexual wishes. Their positive presence was demonstrated in forepleasures and the social existence of obvious perverts walking the streets, filling the hospitals and the courtrooms. These perversions — 'deviations in respect of sexual object', including homosexuality and bestiality, and 'deviations in respect of sexual aim', whereby pleasure extended beyond genitality — represented the re-emergence of component instincts to which we are all heirs. In the universal polymorphous perversity and bisexuality of infancy Freud was able to find roots of what later sociologists were to label as 'our common deviance':

No healthy person, it appears, can fail to make some addition that might be called perverse to the normal sexual aim; and the universality of this finding is in itself enough to show how inappropriate it is to use the word perversion as a term of reproach. [7]

But if this is the case, why retain the concept? The attitude of psycho-analysis to homosexuality is revealing here for the very reason that for Freud it was, as he put it, 'scarcely a perversion'. As a result it has become conventional among some contemporary radical defenders of psycho-analysis to remove homosexuality completely from the category of the perverse, while retaining the category itself. But the real interest in Freud's discussion of the topic, in various forms over many years, is his very real ambiguity and reluctance to do this.

On the one hand, Freud carefully examines and rejects conventional sexological views on the subject. He argues that the reduction in the choice of partner to one of the same sex in homosexuality parallels a similar reduction in heterosexuality. As a result, he suggests, 'from the point of view of psycho-analysis the exclusive sexual interest felt by men for women is also a problem that needs elucidating . . .' [8]. Homosexuality could not be regarded as a thing apart. In the fact of object choice and genital organization of sexual activity it was often continuous with heterosexuality. Moreover, he wrote in his essay on Leonardo, everyone is capable of homosexual object choice, as the evidence of dreams and fantasies reveals. And homosexual feelings, 'blocked and rechannelled', sublimated into more amorphous emotions of solidarity, brotherhood and sisterhood, were an important element in understanding group psychology. All single sex institutions, from the sanctity of priestly orders and peace of monasteries and nunneries, to the masculine ethos of military discipline, might in some sense be seen as resting on sublimated homosexuality [9]. Freud therefore distanced himself from any idea that homosexuality was a sign of 'degener-acy' — a favoured nineteenth-century term — on the grounds that this was no more than a 'a judgement of value, a condemnation instead of an explanation'. He also rejected the distinction, favoured by Havelock Ellis amongst others, between 'acquired' and 'congenital' homosexuality as being 'fruitless and inappropriate' [10]. Homosexuality, like its sibling form heterosexuality, can only be understood in relation to the working of the psychic apparatus as a whole. Its roots were to be found in the universal bisexuality to which we are born, and in the mental processes by which each individual negotiated the hazards of castration anxiety and the Oedipus crisis to obtain a precarious 'sexual identity'.

So, homosexuality was not a disease. It needed no 'cure'. It was widespread. It was continuous with heterosexuality in many of its forms. And like this, it was not a single condition, but more a grouping of different activities, needs and desires:

> What we have thrown together, for reasons of convenience, under the name of homosexuality, may derive from a diversity of processes of psycho-social inhibitions.[11]

Here, apparently, once and for all, we see homosexuality demystified. No longer need it be hidden under a stone like worms and other disturbing creatures. It was a more or less ordinary phenomenon, part of the life of us all, and now subjected to the light of scientific reason. And yet, and yet . . . that is not quite how it has been seen within psychoanalysis, nor was it in practice how ultimately Freud himself was able to leave the subject. The problem is encapsulated in the word 'inhibition'. For while on the one hand we have this rational deconstruction of homosexuality, on the other we are offered a model of sexuality which assumes a normal pattern of development, and which therefore makes homosexuality highly problematic as a life choice. In his famous letter to the mother of a young homosexual, Freud assured her that homosexuality was no vice or degradation, nor was it an illness: it was nothing to be ashamed of. But, he added: 'We consider it to be a variation of the sexual function produced by a certain arrest of the sexual development' [12]. Therein lies the difficulty. A 'development' assumes an appropriate end result, and 'arrest' an artificial blockage. For Freud the growth of each individual from infancy to mature adult sexuality repeated the (hypothetical) development of the race as a whole from primitive sexual promiscuity and perversity to monogamous heterosexuality. This was not a product simply of evolution but of cultural imperatives. It was the tragic destiny of humankind to necessarily forgo the infinite range of the desires in order to ensure survival in a world of scarcity. Each individual, like the race itself, had to attain the 'tyranny of genital organisation' in order to survive, while appropriate object choice became less an act of volition and more a cultural demand. In the end, therefore, a heterosexual and reproductive imperative is reinserted into Freud's account. Once a goal directed version of sexuality is introduced, however surreptitiously, then the whole laboriously constructed edifice of sexual variety begins to totter.

For Freud, the term 'perversion' had a precise technical meaning, as an aspect of all our lives we could not escape. It was a problem only when it became an end in itself and blocked the road to 'mature sexuality'. But it was very difficult to separate that meaning from the wider moral and political meanings attached to it. A crack was left in the door which allowed judgemental values to re-enter a supposedly neutral clinical discourse. Many post-Freudians eagerly pushed the door wide open.

So, for example, Ernest Jones, one of Freud's most loyal supporters and his biographer, criticized him for an over-tolerant attitude to his lesbian patient and commented that 'much is gained if the path to heterosexual gratification is opened . . .'. Later Freudians, in their haste to abandon the idea that homosexuality itself was not a pathology, have even junked Freud's central concept of universal bisexuality. For Socarides, heterosexuality was the natural state from which homosexuality was a deviation. He observes that one of the curious resistances of his patients lay in their assumption that their disorder was 'a normal form of sexuality', and suggests that 'these views must be dealt with from the very beginning'. For Elizabeth Moberly, 'heterosexuality is the goal of human development . . .' [13]. In such comments we can see a return to a pre-Freudian moralism. Freud himself can scarcely be blamed for this. Nevertheless the seeds of such positions are sown by the ambiguities of Freud's own writings. He speaks, at various times, of homosexuality as an abnormality, a disorder, as pathological, and in the male case a 'flight from women'. Indeed, occasionally he even described it without ambiguity as 'a perversion'. Nor is this ultimately surprising. In the last resort, whatever the qualifications in the statement that the germ of perversion is present in us all, the notion of development must imply a norm.

The founders of sexology — and here Freud, one of its most radical figures, was no exception — constructed a unitary model of sexuality from which it has been difficult to escape. On the one hand we are offered a norm of behaviour, which is heterosexual, procreative and largely male, in which female sexuality has almost invariably been defined as secondary or responsive to the male's. (This applies, it must be added, even to the concept of perversion itself. As Plummer has put it, the field of sexual deviation has mainly been demarcated by the issue of male desire [14]. Female breaches with the norm are fitted into a dichotomized picture of male activity and female passivity. Not surprisingly, the most commonly recognized female sexual deviations include servicing men in prostitution or pornography, or 'provoking' men, as in alleged accounts of rape; and lesbianism, the most common form of female sexual variations, has generally been speculated about in terms which derive entirely from the male.) On the other hand, there is an ever-growing catalogue of perversions, deviations, paraphilias, call them what you will, which inevitably marginalizes and in the last resort pathologizes other sexualities. The language of perversion divides the sexual world into the normal and the abnormal, the elect and the damned, and rarely do they meet.

THE DISCOURSE OF DIVERSITY

'The notion of diversity', Ken Plummer has written, 'attempts to capture a more benign and tolerant mood which has recently emerged in pockets of Western culture' [15]. It has to be said that terms like pervert and perversion have not slipped entirely, or even significantly, from public consciousness. In a social and political context where popular support can still be generated for New Right moral crusades by sharp attacks on the sexually unorthodox ('we love the pervert but hate the perversion') it would be difficult to argue that we have moved into a culture which readily accepts sexual variety. 'Pockets' indeed! But in two critical areas, one theoretical, the other political, a 'discourse of diversity' has arisen, and it has had significant cultural effects.

The first area is that of sexology itself. On one level it is little more than a cosmetic terminological change, signalled as early as the 1930s by Havelock Ellis himself. The term 'perversion', he suggested, 'is completely antiquated and mischievous and should be avoided' [16]. He offered as a replacement the less fevered (if still ideologically laden) term, 'sexual deviation', and this phrase has become commonplace in sociological discussions over the past forty years. Latent in such shifts of terminology was a more important change: the recognition of sexual pluralism and the emergence of what Gayle Rubin has described as the concept of a 'benign sexual variation' [17].

The seeds of this new approach were clearly planted by the investigations of the founding sexologists themselves, and the delicate plants were nourished by an appropriation of the Freudian advocacy of a common infantile polymorphous perversity. The celebration of desire as many-sided and many-shaped by some modern writers has taken this position to its logical, often morally anarchic, conclusion. The key figure in transforming the public debate, apart from Freud, was Kinsey. Coming close as he rather reluctantly admitted, to Freud's speculations, he suggested that there was an important idea that rarely featured prominently in either general or scientific discussion, that sex was a normal biological function, acceptable in whatever form it appeared: he wrote to a boy struggling with homosexual feelings, 'Biologically there is no form of outlet which I will admit as abnormal. There is no right or wrong biologically' [18]. Such statements were clearly still in the naturalistic framework of the sexual tradition and in that form must be taken with a pinch of scepticism. Their echoes are more likely to be found today in the speculations of those sociobiologists who profess to see a genetic functionalism in sexual variations than in the writings of sociologists or historians. Yet the underlying message has become crucial to contemporary debates. Few sexologists in the mainstream would feel relaxed at using a term like 'perversion' to describe the varieties of sexual patterns today. For one of the most recent influential studies on the subject, by Robert Stoller, perversion is 'the erotic form of hatred', defined not so much by the acts (*the* perversions) but by the content, hostility, while the term 'pervert' for describing a particular type of person is banned completely from sexological debates. There is even a new and welcome modesty abroad, admitting that '. . . it is crucial to remember that we still know very little about the mechanisms or causes of human sexual behaviour . . .' [19]. Such modesty works against categorical positions.

But if we know little about the causes, we do know increasingly about the forms and frequent occurrence of sexual diversity, and this rather than his questionable biologism is Kinsey's real contribution. The two vast volumes he largely wrote, *Sexual Behavior in the Human Male* and *Sexual Behavior in the Human Female,* and the others he inspired, may have had methodological problems and insufficiently representative samples, and are suffused with unconscious biases of their own. But the thousands of subjects he and his colleagues interviewed provided an unparalleled insight into American sexual life. When it became possible to say, on the basis of what is still the most thorough investigation ever done, that 37 per cent of the male sample had had sexual contact to orgasm with another male, then even if the sample was unrepresentative and the percentage figures were exaggerated, homosexual activity could no longer be seen as a morbid symptom of a tiny, sick minority. At least amongst a significant section of American life it was a fairly common occurrence. And if this was true of homosexuality, then it was potentially true also for a wide range of other sexualities, from bestiality to paedophilia, from sado-masochism to a passion for pornography. Kinsey was fascinated by the range of variations in human sexual behaviours. He cited with glee the example of two men who lived in the same town, met at the same place of business, had common social activities, and yet experienced in enormously different sexual lives. One individual he interviewed had had one ejaculation in thirty years; another had thirty a week, a difference of 45,000 times. This was just one example for Kinsey of the vast variety that existed, across the divide of class, gender and race. From this flowed a profoundly important and influential sociological — and political — point. He wrote:

> The publicly pretended code of morals, our social organization, our marriage customs, our sex laws, and our educational and religious systems are based upon an assumption that individuals are much alike sexually and that it is an equally simple matter for all of them to confine their behavior to the single pattern which the mores dictate. [20]

But what if people were in fact different, had different needs, desires and behaviour? Then a yawning gap would appear between moral codes and sexual behaviour, throwing into confusion the absolutist certainties of the sexual tradition. This was the favoured point of departure for subsequent critiques of normative regulations.

If transformations within mainstream sexology provided a theoretical framework for a recognition of diversity, the political energy came from a different source, that of the sexual minorities themselves. We noted earlier that since at least the nineteenth-century most industrial societies have witnessed a sustained effort to articulate and develop distinct lesbian and male homosexual identities in the context of extending subcultures and social communities. As the homosexual ways of life have become more public and self-confident, so in their wake other assertions of minority sexual identities have emerged. The example of homosexuality, as Gayle Rubin has argued, has provided a repertoire of political strategies and organizational forms for the mobilization of other erotic populations [21]. Transvestites, transsexuals, paedophiles, sado-masochists, fetishists, bisexuals, prostitutes and others have vocally emerged, clamouring for their right of self-expression and legitimacy. The hesitantly speaking perverts of Krafft-Ebing's medico-forensic pages, confessing their most intimate secrets to the new sexual experts, have walked out of the clinical text and onto the stage of history, the living proof of sexual diversity.

These new sexual and social identities may have emerged on the terrain first mapped and carefully articulated by the sexologists themselves. But as Kinsey himself forcefully observed, it is only the human mind which invents categories and tries to force facts into separate pigeonholes; and the facts constantly subvert.

Sexology was important in establishing the language by which these miscreants were described and analysed. Through their symbiotic relationship with the medical profession (many of them, like Ellis, were trained doctors), these early sexologists helped construct a very influential disease model, the effects of which are still with us. But the poor creatures they described were not their inventions: they were products of very complex social processes, of social definition and of self-definition in which sexology played an important but not decisive part. Moreover, the language of sexology could itself be used to challenge the certainties of the sexual tradition.

I started this chapter with words. Three other words symbolize the move taking place: 'sodomite', 'homosexual', 'gay'. Just as the widespread emergence (at first in America) of the self-description 'gay' in the 1950s and 1960s marked a crucial new stage in the emergence of a politicized sexual identity, the gradual spread of the term 'homosexual' from the late nineteenth century marked a significant breach with the traditional termi-nology of the sin that could not be named amongst Christians, that of sodomy. 'Sodomite' was a term suffused with heavy tones of mediaeval morality. It was also ambiguous. It signified some one who committed a particular type of sexual act, that of buggery or anal intercourse. The homosexual, on the other hand, was a particular type of sexual person, given not only a name but a personalized history (weak father, strong mother, or sometimes overbearing father and submissive mother), physical characteristics (wide hips and high voice if a man, masculinized figure and hair on the upper lip if a woman), and indicative failures (inability to whistle, dislike of children). Many thus described by the clinical discourse might not recognize themselves fully or at all in such descriptions; but they were able to validate their existence, affirm that others like them existed by their naming, and that, far from being unique creatures, they could re-enter the canons of recognized, if perverted, sexualities. A new language of self-description emerged — 'invert', 'uranian', 'third' or 'intermediate' sex — that marked the embryonic stirring of an affirmative, and modern, sense of self.

The search for valid sexual identities has characterized the history of homosexuality, male and female, during this century. Different groups of people have found different ways of doing this: there is no pre-ordained goal. Gender, geographical and racial differences have produced differen-tiated identities. But a firm identity remains, it seems, essential. Categori-zation and self-labellings, that is the process of working out a social identity, may control, restrict and inhibit, as many critics have argued, but at the same time it provides, as Plummer has noted, 'comfort, security and assuredness' [22]; and a precondition for attaining a secure sense of personal identity and belonging has been the development of wider social networks, of finding a collective way of dealing with sexual differentiation, of establishing sexual communities.

The emergence of distinctive sexual subcultures and communities is part of a wider process that has marked the twentieth century, that of ever-growing social complexity and social differentiation, producing a new pluralism of class, ethnic, racial and cultural forms as well as a diversity of gender and sexual experiences. This process of differentiation has of course produced not only complexity but new forms of social conflict and antago- nism. It is in the context of continuing struggle over appropriate behaviour that politicized sexual identities have also emerged, articulated since the late nineteenth century in a series of homosexual rights groupings and other sex reform movements throughout the industrialized world. These have been an important way of minorities responding to the changing patterns of sexual regulation and of challenging sexual norms.

Five factors seem to be necessary for this successful emergence [23]: the existence of large numbers in the same situation; geographical concent- ration; identifiable targets of opposition; sudden events or changes in social position; and an intellectual leadership with readily understood goals. Each of these has been present in the history of homosexual movements at various times, which explains its significant social presence compared to other sexual minorities. Already by the late nineteenth century there were large numbers of men who saw themselves as homosexual and they were increasingly constructing subcultures. Lesbian groupings were more embryonic; nevertheless, in many North American and European cities both an identity and social networks were developing. These were the seedbeds of support for such organizations as Magnus Hirschfeld's Scienti-. fic–Humanitarian Committee in Germany, founded in 1898, and the smaller sex reform organizations in Britain and elswhere, founded on the eve of the First World War. The organizations fluctuated in their fortunes as political circumstances changes. The German homosexual movement, at one time the largest in the world, was effectively destroyed by the Nazis during the 1930s. By the 1950s nevertheless there was a new initiative, this time based in the United States of America. Organizations like the Mattachine society and the Daughters of Bilitis were founded partly in the wake of the McCarthyite witch hunts against sexual deviants in the early 1950s, but also in the context of expanding subcultures of male homosex- uals and lesbians during the post-war decade. It was the juncture of the increasingly sophisticated gay communities of cities like New York and San Francisco with a newly politicized movement of 'gay liberationists' in the late 1960s that provided the energy for the emergence of mass gay and lesbian movements in the USA in the 1970s and 1980s. This provided a model which other countries followed wherever local conditions permitted.

Conditions that made it possible for homosexuality to find a voice have not always been present for other groupings. The intense stigma attached to paedophilia (sexual attraction to children) and its controversial, if con- tested, overlap with child sex abuse has made it very difficult for its advocates to develop a substantial subculture, find a common voice or group together over long periods in stable organizations. Characteristic organizations like NAMBLA (North America Man Boy Love Association) in the United States and PIE (Paedophile Information Exchange) in Britain have experienced social obloquy and constant police attention even for advocating changed attitudes. Perhaps more crucially, it is not an activity that lends itself easily to the establishment of stable social communities, given the social hostility and the transient nature of many paedophile relations, stemming from the fact that children tend to grow up, and the disparity in interest between adults and children. Advocates of sado-masochistic sexual activity (SM) are also limited in number, which inhibits the establishment of large-scale movements, though they have developed support networks and small-scale subcultures in various Western cities. SM has also become an issue of major sexual political controversy in various radical movements, with both the feminist and gay and lesbian movements sharply divided about the merits of such activities. Issues related to transvestites and transsexuals have also split these movement, though controversies in these cases have not been so much about sexual activity as about their claimed perpetuation of existing gender stereotypes. Prostitutes and other sex workers (in pornography, strip clubs, etc.) have posed different problems again for political organization: about the validity of working in the commercial sexual field and about women servicing male fantasies, which often involve the playing out of desires for violence and degradation.

But although the conditions for the emergence of powerful political organizations on the model of gay and lesbian groupings may vary, the fact is that through the industrialized world, and possibly as a result of industrialization and urbanization, new 'communities of interest' have emerged around sexual issues, and through these a range of sexual identities have been affirmed. There no longer appears to be a great continent of normality surrounded by small islands of disorder. Instead we can now witness hugh clusters of islands, great and small, which seem in constant motion one to the other, each with its own unique vegetation and geography. New categories and erotic minorities have emerged. Older ones have experienced a process of subdivision as specialized tastes, specific aptitudes and needs become the basis for proliferating sexual identities: 'swinging' couples, 'butch and fem' lesbians, SM gays, leather dykes and denim queens . . . . The list is potentially endless as each specific desire becomes a locus of political statement and possible social identity.

A number of questions inevitably arise: is each form of desire of equal validity; should each subdivision of desire be the basis of a sexual and possible social identity; is each claim for identity of equal weight in the debates of sexual politics; what about the heterosexual identity? And if we reject the category of the perverse altogether in favour of a celebratory discourse of diversity, are there any means by which we can distinguish the good from the bad, the appropriate from the inappropriate and, dare we say it, the moral from the immoral? To affirm the existence of diversity does not answer difficult question posed by the sexual tradition: it merely raises new ones.

DECONSTRUCTING THE CATEGORIES

The first point to make is that the admitted *fact* of sexual diversity need not lead to a *norm* of diversity. The efforts made by social moralists to encourage or enforce a return to 'traditional values' suggests that some people at least have not given up the hope of a revival of a universal moral standard. Nor are such absolutist hopes confined to the sexually conservative. There are powerful tendencies amongst some feminists, sex radicals and more generally on parts of the Left to search for a 'new morality' in which the corrupt elements of a capitalist/bourgeois/male-dominated/ heterosexist/society — the language varies — could be finally eliminated. The problem here lies in the fact that even amongst the sexually oppressed and vocal sexual minorities there is little agreement. Is pornography constitutive of male violence, or a reflection of a generally sexist society, or harmless? Is inter-generational sex a radical challenge to arbitrary divisions of age, or is it child sex abuse? Is transsexuality a challenge to the tyranny of gender sterotypes or is it a surrender to such sexual divisions and stereotypes? Does sado-masochism involve a submersion in dangerous fantasies of violence, or is it no more than a harmless playing out of eroticized power relations? These questions and many others have become key ones in the ranks of sexual politics in recent years. They are important, because they challenge us to rethink the criteria by which we are able to decide between appropriate and inappropriate behaviour.

The sexual tradition has basically offered two positions: either sex is fundamentally dangerous, acceptable only when channelled into appropriate channels (generally, marital procreative sex); or sex is basically healthy and good, but it has been repressed, distorted and denied by a corrupt society. There is a third approach, which is the one I have advocated in this essay: that sex only attains meaning in social relations, which implies that we can only make appropriate choices around sexuality by understanding its social and political context. This involves a decisive move away from the morality of 'acts' which has dominated sexual theorizing for hundreds of years and in the direction of a new relational perspective which takes into account context and meanings. We still take it for granted that sin or salvation, morality or immorality, normality or abnormality reside in what we do. This was enshrined in the Christian codes of the Middle Ages, in the tables that declared that heterosexual rape was higher up the scale of value than masturbation or consensual sodomy, because the former was procreative and the latter were barren. There, the priority given to reproduction dictated the hierarchy of value. In the late twentieth century we are ostensibly more tolerant, but we still take for granted the assumption that some practices are inherently better than others. Now, however, we tend to give credit to nature, or biology, or the science of sex for revealing this hierarchy. Anal intercourse is no longer the worst crime known to Christians — though it is still technically illegal in Britain amongst married couples. Masturbation is encouraged by books, magazines and papers on every station bookstall. Sometimes this escalator effect is because of scientific reassessment. More usually it is the result of moral and political changes helped by well-organized campaigns. It was the militant organization of homosexuals that led to the removal of homosexuality from the list of diseases of the American Psychiatric Association in 1974 [24]. Passionate campaigns by feminists and social purity men and women over the past hundred years have shifted perceptions of inter-generational sex, pornography and prostitution in various directions. But the unconscious belief that some acts are better than others still exists, even if, in a pluralistic world, we cannot always agree what that order ought to be.

A relational perspective attempts, on the other hand, to understand all these sexual practices as aspects of wider social relations, to unravel the context in which acts become meaningful. This in turn involves attempting to understand the power relations at play, the subtle coercions which limit the possibilities of choice, the likely impact of a particular sexual activity on the self and others, as well as the possibilities of pleasure and personal autonomy that may be encouraged. There are very difficult issues at stake in such an endorsement of moral pluralism, and I shall attempt to explore these later. The point that needs underlining here is that such a perspective must involve breaking with any moral system based on acts as such.

There is, however, perhaps an even more challenging implication. In the sexual tradition certain acts have been seen as living examples of a particular sexual system, manifestations of a syndrome. The perspective embryonically outlined here breaks with such unitary categories. If we do this it will no longer be possible to condemn a sexual practice because it is 'homosexual' or even 'heterosexual', 'sado-masochistic' or 'paedophile'. Instead we should begin to ask: what makes this particular activity valid or invalid, appropriate or inappropriate? What are the social factors that make these meaningful? What are the power relations at work?

If we take three examples we will see the type of factors that must be taken into account. The first example is of heterosexuality. At first sight this may seem surprising. Heterosexuality is so much taken for granted as the norm that it is rarely questioned. It is the given of sexual theorizing, the natural form by which we judge others. But a little more patience, as well as an attentive reading of the literature of sex, would show that it is not a single phenomenon. The term embraces rape as well as loving relationships, coercion as well as choice. It covers a multitude of sexual practices from intercourse in the missionary position to oral and anal intercourse. As a term it obscures differences of age, of institutionalization and even of the fantasies of the partners involved. In itself it describes nothing except the fact of object choice. The meanings of this may be diverse. But if the privileging of heterosexuality obscures real differences, then similarly a total rejection of it is more than misguided. Some feminist critics of its current form have ended up by rejecting all forms of heterosexuality because it supposedly perpetuates male dominance. For writers such as Adrienne Rich 'compulsory heterosexuality' is the key mechanism of control of women, and hence heterosexuality becomes *the* enemy [25]. This position is simply the mirror image of our cultural privileging of heterosexuality. A relational perspective would start out not with the object choice or the act (genital intercourse) which is taken as its most characteristic form, but with the host of factors that shape its significance. Does the possibility exist for equal relations between the man and woman? If not, is the sexual act itself one means of perpetuating relations of domination and subordination? If so, what are the alternatives? Is change necessary or even desirable? Such are the questions posed by a rethinking of heterosexuality.

The power relations that sex can involve are most dramatically illustrated by the question of sex between the generations. For the vast majority of the population this is not a serious issue as such, it is simply child sex abuse. It involves powerful adults using their experience and wiles to gain satisfaction from inexperienced and vulnerable children. For advocates of paedophilia on the other hand, there is a mirror-image celebration of the possibilities of inter-generational sex. It is applauded for its pedagogic possibilities — the so-called Greek love justification: in the passage from childhood dependence to adult responsibility, guidance, sexual and moral, of a caring man can be invaluable, it is argued. It is further legitimated by the supposed facts of childhood sexuality: sexology itself has revealed the wide extent of childhood sexual potentiality including the existence of infantile masturbation. If something is so natural, and omnipresent, should it be as rigidly controlled as childhood sexuality is today? And again, if it is natural, then surely it cannot be harmful even if it takes place with adults. As Tom

O'Carroll has written '. . . there is no need whatever for a child to know "the consequences" of engaging in harmless sex play, simply because it is exactly that: harmless' [26].

Rather than engage in such either/or arguments, it is more rational, I suggest, to look again at what is involved. And if we do this, we should not be surprised if we can find a variety of different elements that could be disaggregated. The first one is that of age. Is there an ideal age at which consent becomes free, and a relationship becomes consensual? Certainly the vast majority of us could agree that it should not be 3 or 8, but what about 12, which seems to be the norm in some cultures, and which late in 1985 a conservative-led Dutch government proposed should be their age of consent, or 14 or 15 which are the ages of consent in various European countries? Laws vary enormously and affect boys and girls quite differently (in Britain the age of consent for girls is 16, for male homosexuals 21, and for other men it seems to hover uncertainly around the age of 16). This points to the potential importance of questions of gender in assessing paedophilia. It has been suggested, for instance, that girls, because of their potential fertility and their cultural status as sexual playthings, are more vulnerable than boys in relations with adults. And is it important to make a distinction between homosexual and heterosexual paedophilia because homosexual relations may lack some of the power imbalances of heterosexual relations? It has also been argued that the initiatory role of children is ignored in debates on paedophilia: there is some evidence that sexual activity is often instigated by young people themselves. Does this make inter-generational sex more valid or is it completely irrelevant to our decision making? Brian Taylor has pointed to the existence of eight possible subcategories of inter-generational sex, depending on the age of those involved, the distinction of gender, the nature of the sexual proclivity, and the interaction of all three [27]. This suggests that there are paedophilias, not a single paedophilia. At the end of the day we might still want to condemn all forms as child sex abuse. But we should no longer do this simply because it is a single activity; rather we have to bring in other criteria which are not intrinsic to the sexual act itself.

Power is an acute issue in discussions of inter-generational sex. In consensual sado-masochism this is taken a step further, to the eroticization of power itself: 'we select the most frightening, disgusting or unacceptable activities and transmute them into pleasure' [28]. For the theorists of the sexual tradition, SM had its roots in an exaggeration of the normal relations intrinsic between men and women. For Krafft-Ebing, sadism was 'nothing else than excessive and monstrous pathological intensification of phenomena — possible too in normal conditions, in rudimental forms — which accompany the psychical sexual life, particularly in males — . . . .Masochism is the opposite of sadism . . .' [29]. Yet for many advocates of SM from within the sexual subcultures of the West, it provides unique insights into the nature of sexual power, therapeutic and cathartic sex revealing the nature of sex as ritual and play [30]. Such claims are no doubt exaggerated, but what they effectively do is pose very dramatically the question of the relationship between context and choice, subjectivity and consent in thinking about sexuality. Should people have the right to consent to activities that are conventionally regarded as painful and potentially harmful? What are the conditions that make such choices valid? Is there the same possibility of free choice between say a man and a woman as there is between people of 'the same caste' (gay, two women)? The activities of the 'sexual fringe', of which SMers are perhaps the most radically transgressive members, may remain marginal to the mainstream of most people's sexual lives, but they do in fact ask major questions about what are the limits of normality, what are the boundaries of valid sexual activity, and what are the extremes to which we should go in the pursuit of pleasure.

A disaggregation of sexual practices along the lines I propose here opens them up to social and political interrogation. Inevitably we will not find simple answers for and against particular activities in doing this. But deconstructing the unitary categories of the sexologists has the inestimable value of opening up crucial debates about the parameters within which valid decisions and choices can be made.

Two final points need to be made. First of all, the acceptance of the idea that there are benign social variations must not imply an abandonment of distinctions. There are certain classes of act connected with sex that can find universal condemnation as malignant, especially those involving deliberate acts of violence, whether in the form of sexual murder, rape, or child abuse. This is the class that Stoller appears to be addressing in his attempt to theorize perversion as the erotic form of hatred. It is a potentiality in all of us, in his view, which relates to the tensions and anxieties produced by the necessity of attaining particular gender identities. There may well be scope for the development of theoretical insights into the nature of aberrant activities in this way — though that is a question that needs to be left to another place, another time. The issue that needs stressing is that, even here, it is not the act itself which constitutes the problem but the whole context — social and psychic — that gives rise to it, and from which it takes its meaning; factors such as family circumstances or male anxiety and power. In other words, if the perversion in this sophisticated psychoanalytic approach is in fact a revolt against the limits imposed by culture, a means of eluding, in Chasseguet-Smirgel's phrase, 'the fatal character of the Oedipus complex' [31], a life-denying leap away from reality, then it is still that culture, that reality which can help us to understand the individual activity.

The traditional concentration on the aetiology of the individual's act can no longer be sufficient. This leads to the second point, concerning the real meaning of the concept of diversity. As Plummer has said:

> however neutral and objective talk about sexual diversity appears to be, it is also talk about *power*. Every culture has to establish — through both formal and informal political processes — the range and scope of the diversities that will be outlawed or banned. No culture could function with a sexual free-for-all, but the pattern of these constraints is exceedingly variable across time and space. [32]

The vital point here is that the distinctions we make are in the last resort ethical or political ones, dependent less on the rational weighing of evidence than on the political balance of forces. It is for this reason that questions of sexuality are inevitably, inescapably, political questions. What is ultimately wrong with the term 'perversion' is that its ostensibly scientific terminology obscures moral and political judgements. It forecloses debate. The advantage of embracing the term 'diversity' is that it leaves the important questions wide open — to debate, negotiation, and political choice.

REFERENCES

[1] Gayle Rubin, 'Thinking sex: notes for a radical theory of the politics of sexuality', in Carole S. Vance (ed.), *Pleasure and Danger. Exploring Female Sexuality,* Routledge & Kegan Paul, Boston and London (1984), p. 287.

[2] Havelock Ellis, *The Psychology of Sex,* William Heinenmann, London (1946; first published 1933), p. 126.

[3] Alfred C. Kinsey, Wardell B. Pomeroy and Clyde E. Martin, *Sexual Behavior in the Human Male,* W. B. Saunders, Philadelphia and London (1948), p. 202.

[4] Michel Foucault, *The History of Sexuality,* Vol. 1, *An Introduction* trans. Robert Hurley, Allen Lane, London (1979).

[5] J. Laplanche and J. B. Pontalis, *The Language of Psychoanalysis,* The Hogarth Press and the Institute of Psychoanalysis, London (1980), p. 307.

[6] Sigmund Freud, 'The sexual aberrations', in *Three Essays on the Theory of Sexuality, Standard Edition,* Vol. 7.

[7] Ibid., p. 160.

[8] Ibid., p. 146, note 1, added 1915.

[9] Sigmund Freud, *Leonardo da Vinci and a Memory of his Childhood* (1910), *Standard Edition*, Vol. II, p. 99, footnote; *Group Psychology and the Analysis of the Ego, Standard Edition,* Vol. 18, pp. 67–143.

[10] *Three Essays,* pp. 138–139; 'Homosexuality in a woman', *Standard Edition,* Vol. 18, p. 154.

[11] *Three Essays,* p. 146.

[12] Ernst Freud (ed.), *Letters of Sigmund Freud* 1873–1939, Hogarth Press, London (1961), p. 277.

[13] Ernest Jones, *The Life and Work of Sigmund Freud,* Vol. 2, Basic Books, New York (1955), p. 299, C. W. Socarides, *Homosexuality,* Jason Aranson, New York (1978); Elizabeth R. Moberly, *Psychoanalysis. The Early Development of Gender-identity,* Routledge & Kegan Paul, London (1983), p. x.

[14] Kenneth Plummer, 'Sexual diversity: a sociological perspective', in K. Howells (ed.), *Sexual Diversity,* Blackwell, Oxford (1984), p. 219.

[15] Ibid., p. 221.

[16] Havelock Ellis, *The Psychology of Sex,* p. 127.

[17] Gayle Rubin, 'Thinking sex: notes for a radical theory of the politics of sexuality' in Carole S. Vance (ed.), *Pleasure and Danger.*

[18] Wardell, B. Pomeroy, *Dr Kinsey and the Institute for Sex Research,* Harper & Row, New York (1972), p. 77.

[19] Robert J. Stoller, *Perversion. The Erotic Form of Hatred,* Quartet, London (1977), p. 45.

[20] Kinsey *et al., Sexual Behavior in the Human Male,* p. 197.

[21] Rubin, op.cit.

[22] Kenneth Plummer (ed.), *The Making of the Modern Homosexual,* Hutchinson, London (1980), p. 29.

[23] See Barry Adam, *The Survival of Domination, Inferiorisation and Everyday Life,* Elsevier, New York, Oxford (1978); John D'Emilio, *Sexual Politics, Sexual Communities. The Making of a Homosexual Minority in the United States 1940–1970,* University of Chicago Press, Chicago, London (1983).

[24] Ronald Bayer, *Homosexuality and American Psychiatry. The Politics of Diagnosis,* Basic Books, New York (1981). On similar moves in Australia see R. F. Barr *et al.,* 'Homosexuality and psychological adjustment', *The Medical Journal of Australia,* **1,** 1984.

[25] Adrienne Rich, 'Compulsory heterosexuality and lesbian existence', in Ann Snitow, Christine Stansell and Sharon Thompson (eds.), *Desire: The Politics of Sexuality,* Virago, London (1984).

[26] Tom O'Carroll, *Paedophilia. The Radical Case,* Peter Owen, London (1980), p. 153. For the various legitimations offered see the discussion

in Ken Plummer, 'The paedophile's progress', in Brian Taylor (ed.), *Perspectives on paedophilia,* Batsford, London (1981).

[27] See Brian Taylor's 'Introduction' in Taylor (ed.), op.cit.

[28] Pat Califia, 'Unraveling the sexual fringe. A secret side of lesbian sexuality', *The Advocate,* 27 Dec. 1979, p. 19.

[29] Thomas Weinberg and G. W. Levi Kamel (eds.), *S and M. Studies in Sado Masochism,* Prometheus Books, Buffalo, NY (1983), p. 27.

[30] For a strong defence of SM see Samois (ed.), *Coming to Power. Writings and Graphics on Lesbian S/M,* Samois, Berkeley, Ca (1982); for an opposing view see Robin Ruth Linden *et al.* (eds.), *Against Sadomasochism. A Radical Feminist Analysis,* Frog in the Web, East Palo Alto, Ca. (1982).

[31] Janine Chasseguet-Smirgel, *Creativity and Perversion,* Free Association Books, London (1985), p. 26.

[32] Plummer, 'Sexual Diversity', p. 219.

5

Sexuality and Politics

> . . . there is no aspect of human behaviour about which there has been more thought, more talk, and more books written.
>
> Alfred Kinsey [1]

SEX: A NEW FRONT LINE?

Concern with sexuality has been at the heart of Western preoccupations since before the triumph of Christianity. It has been a matter of political debate for something like two hundred years. Already, by the last decades of the nineteenth century, the preoccupations of contemporary feminism were on the agenda: concerning male power over women, sexual exploitation, the differences between men and women and the meaning of consent and choice. By the 1920s and 1930s, with the rise and fall of a world sex reform movement, and the apparently irresistible rise and rise of social authoritarianism and fascism, the intricate connections between sexual values and political power were clearly visible. It was during this period, through the writings of such people as Wilhelm Reich, that a concept connecting sex and politics — 'sexual politics' — first came into being.

It is fair to say, nevertheless, that only since the 1960s has the idea of sexual politics had any real impact and resonance, moving from the periphery to the centre. Today we take it for granted as a powerful contemporary reality: the phrase has become almost a cliché, yet its ramifications run through the whole of modern social life and politics. Moreover, it is no longer a politics confined to what can broadly be called 'the left' or 'progressive' circles. During the 1970s and early 1980s some of the most skilful and influential developments of a politics around sexuality have come from conservative forces, especially those grouped under the umbrella label of the 'New Right'. To an unexpected and unusual degree, sexuality has become a battleground for contending political forces, a new front-line, in Dennis Altman's graphic phrase, of contemporary politics [2]. It seems that for many the struggle for the future of society must be fought on the terrain of contemporary sexuality. As sexuality goes, so goes society.

This intense preoccupation with the erotic simultaneously grows out of, and contributes to, a developing crisis of sexuality. At its centre is a crisis of the relations between the sexes, profoundly unsettled by rapid social change and by the rise of modern feminism, with its wide-ranging critiques of, and challenges to, the various forms of male domination and female subordination. This is the meaning of 'sexual politics' in its broadest sense: a struggle over the present and future of sexual difference and sexual division. But this in turn feeds a growing crisis over the meaning of sexuality in our culture, about the place we give to sex in our lives and relationships, about identity and pleasure, obligation and power, choice and consent. The fixed points which seemed to organize and regulate our sexual beliefs and morals — religious, familial, heterosexual, monogamous — have been radically challenged during this century. The rule of 'traditional values' may have been partial and ineffective; the norms may have been restrictive and authoritarian. But the apparent eclipse of their hegemony has left a vacuum. We are no longer quite sure — or at least agreed on — what we mean by sexuality, or what its role in social and individual lives should be. There is a new pluralism of beliefs and behaviours abroad, going beyond a diversity of sexual activities to a wide range of patterns of relationships. Perhaps this pluralism was always there, beneath our unsuspecting, moralistic eyes: there is growing historical and sociological evidence to suggest this. Nevertheless, the recognition of sexual and social diversity as a spectacular fact has sharpened the dilemma of how to cope with it in social policy and personal practice. It is this that explains the emergence and impact of what has been called a '*sexual* sexual politics': a prioritization of those issues which have been shaping and reshaping moral debates for well over a hundred years, but whose profile has been frequently obscured or marginalized in mainstream politics.

I referred to 'traditional values'. It seems to be one of the characteristics of people faced by rapid social change to yearn for a return to a supposed 'golden age' of order, decency, discipline and propriety. The difficult is that the more we search for it, the more we seem to find ourselves locked into an endless maze where the goal is always just around the next corner. Was this 'golden age' in the 1950s, before the supposed descent into 'permissiveness' during the 1960s, with what Margaret Thatcher called its denigration of 'the old virtues of discipline and self-restraint'? [3] Or could it be found in the years between the wars, when writers like Marie Stopes looked forward to a 'glorious unfolding' in relations between men and women? Or perhaps we may find traces of it in the last great flowering of peace and social hierarchy before the outbreak of the First World War, if we ignore its materialist excesses and upper-class philanderings? Each of these periods has had its advocates as a 'golden age' — but, more important, each also had their own prophets of decline and doom. Recently a consensus seems to have emerged amongst those who wish to restore 'old standards': surely (in Britain) it is 'Victorian values' that must be sought out and re-established, or (in the USA) the hearty values, where a man was a man and a woman a woman, of the American frontier. The reality, of course, is always a little less glittering. Far from there being a moral consensus in the nineteenth century, it was in many ways a period which mirrors our own: of rapid change, moral dislocation, and a sustained but not over-effective 'grappling for control'. 'Consensus', such as it was, emerged only precariously at the end of the century, an uneasy compromise between moral conviction and political expediency. Not much of a real model there.

The historical accuracy of a reference point in the past is, however, irrelevant to its contemporary power. It provides a yardstick with which to judge the present, usually revealing more about our current discontents than past realities. More particularly, the glorification of the past enables people in the present to pinpoint the imagined movement of decline. If 'Victorian values' represents a positive symbol, 'permissiveness' represents its negative for many contemporary critics, and the 1960s its moment of singular success. The British conservative journalist, Ronald Butt, has written of the triumph of a new liberalism in the 1960s, whose essence was:

> permissiveness in one strictly limited social area (i.e. sex) coupled with the exaction of strict obedience to new norms prescribed by the liberal orthodoxy in another. In some matters, a charter of individual licence was granted which unleashed an unprecedented attack on old commonly held standards of personal behaviour and responsibility. . . . [4]

The interesting point to note about a jeremiad such as this is not so much its strict accuracy — my own conviction is that it is in fact a distortion both of the decade and of the changes that have taken place — as its representative quality. The changes which the decade of the 1960s has come to a stand for — a liberalization of attitudes, greater freedom of sexual discussion, reforms of the law and so on — have become symbolic of all that has gone wrong, the area, as Ernest Whitehouse (husband of the social purity leader Mary Whitehouse) has said, 'in which the biggest breakdown in moral standards has occurred' [5].

It is worth noting that this attack on the 1960s is not confined to the political right. It finds echoes in a disillusioned liberalism which sought satisfaction in a new hedonism, and found instead disillusion; and in a moral feminism which regards the decade as a period in which the increased sexualization of women's bodies led them ever more closely to the thralls of male sexual power. Two points need to be made about such views. First, it is a curious historical distortion to focus all changes on a mythologized decade. Many of the changes that have genuinely occured have had a long gestation. Some postdate the 1960s themselves. Secondly, it is obviously inadequate to see any period as monolithic. The 1960s witnessed not only the increased exploitative deployment of images of female sexuality but also the revival of feminism, not only sex reform but also the rebirth of moral purity campaigns and the search for new forms of regulation. Change is always complex, and if we are to adapt to it, and control it, we need to understand what exactly is at stake and not surrender to myths about the past — or the present.

ELEMENTS OF A SEXUAL CRISIS

So what has changed? I suggest there are three broad areas where change has been rapid, if not entirely, or at all, cataclysmic. The first I shall call the 'secularization' of sex. By this I mean the progressive detachment of sexual values from religious values — even for many of the religious. This has a long history, but possibly the key feature of its development was the process, beginning in the mid-nineteenth century, whereby the initiative for judging sexuality passed from the Churches to the agents of social and mental hygiene, primarily in the medical profession. This has been an unfinished revolution in the sense that moral and medical matters remain inextricably linked. You can still be singled out as sick and immoral if you offend our unspoken norms. Nor, of course, do I intend to imply that the religious have given up their attempts to regulate sex. We only have to observe the rise of religious fundamentalism tied to moral authoritarianism in the Christian and non-Christian worlds to counter that argument. Nevertheless, sexuality has become increasingly the province of non-religious experts — in sexology, psychology, welfare services and social policy, as well as in medicine itself. Even in the most traditional of churches, such as the Roman Catholic, many of the faithful ignore their leaders' teaching on birth control or homosexuality. For the non-religious, attitudes have largely floated free of religious sanctions. The process of secularization has gone further in some countries (Great Britain) than in others (the USA, Ireland, North and South). In all of them, however, the effect has been to place on sexual relations themselves a greater burden of expectation than hitherto. In the absence of any alternative world outlook to religion's, sex itself has become an arena for thinking about personal destiny and belonging.

This tendency has been encouraged, and in part caused by a related process: the ever-increasing involvement of sex and the market, the drawing into commodity relations and relations of exchange of growing areas of 'private life'. The most spectacular example of this has been the vast growth of the market for pornography in the past generation (by the early 1980s it was estimated to be a $5 billion industry in the USA); but these are other, more subtle areas of change. Patterns of courtship have been influenced by the commercialization of leisure — from discos to motor cars. New technologies have shaped various aspects of personal life, from sex aids to reproductive techniques. Sex — especially female sexuality — has become a central feature of advertising, a vital element in the selling of everything from cigarettes to central heating. At the same time, new markets for sexual products have constantly been discovered or created — amongst adolescents in the 1950s, women in the 1960s, gays and lesbians in the 1970s.

These changes have obviously increased the possibilities for exploitation, and their ill-effects can be seen in the form of degrading and objectifying imagery of women, in the seediness of the sex areas of major cities, in a romanticization of sexual violence, and the commercialization of sexual pleasures. But for many millions of people escaping from social privation and sexual authoritarianism this new 'sexual freedom' has offered new possibilities. The changes of the past generations have acted like a solvent an old certainties and inherited values. They have opened the way to new dangers, providing ample scope for the rise of a new moralism. But they have also provided undreamt of opportunities which many have seized.

Not surprisingly — and this is the second major trend — there has been a widespread *liberalization* of attitudes throughout the industrialized West. People are generally more accepting of birth control, abortion, divorce, pre-marital sex, cohabitation of non-married partners and divorce, and of homosexuality. There has been a new recognition of the legitimacy of female sexuality. This does not mean there are not major pockets of difficulty. The Roman Catholic hierarchy throughout the West has continued its opposition to non-marital sex, artificial birth control, abortion and divorce. Homosexuality remains illegal in many states of America and elswhere, and in European countries the law continues to treat homosexuality and heterosexuality differentially in age-of consent laws and so on. Above all, perhaps, the changes have differentially affected men and women. There have been greater opportunities for women to express their sexuality, a major encouragement of female sexual fulfilment. But in a culture which remains resolutely male-dominated, this has often been in situations defined by men, for the benefit of men. Nevertheless, on all standard measures of opinion, attitudes, if not universally non-authoritarian or non-exploitative, are certainly more varied and open than they were in the 1950s and earlier. This has been accompanied by an explosion of discourses around sexuality, a new willingness, and compulsion indeed, to speak about sex, resulting in an unprecedented profusion to sexual debates and addresses in everything from marital handbooks to popular music. Even homosexuality, the love that once dared not speak its name, has assumed an unprecedented volubility, and in its wake other sexual minorities have spoken of their needs and rights in a new vocabulary of sexual desire. 'Sexuality' now speaks in many languages, to and for many different types of people, offering a cacophony of alternative values and possibilities.

The effects of all this on *behaviour* are more difficult to gauge. Certainly, there have been significant changes, particularly in the openness with which sex outside marriage now takes place. In a country like Sweden the vast majority (99 per cent) of both men and women now have sexual relations before they are married; in the USA about 50 per cent of women and rather more men do. Similarly, with extramarital sex, recent surveys suggest perhaps one-third of women, and half of the men, have sexual relations outside the bounds of marriage. Men and women may not be having more sex, but they seem to be doing it more often outside the formal parameters of legal marriage [6].

They also appear to be engaging in sexual activity on average earlier than their parents or grandparents. This is partly a result of earlier maturity in boys and girls (the age of menarche has come down from 16 to 13 in the past 100 years), partly a result of greater opportunity. It has been estimated that the number of girls sexually active under the age of consent of 16 in Britain may have trebled over the past two decades — though there was also evidence that promiscuity was no greater than for their parents' generation. During the 1970s and early 1980s, nevertheless, the issue of teenage sex has become a major one, posing difficult questions concerning sexual knowledge, choice and control. The court action brought by Mrs Victoria Gillick in Britain, to legally prevent doctors giving birth control advice to girls under 16 without parental consent, failed on appeal in October 1985. Nevertheless, the protracted legal action raised critical questions about *who* should decide (parents, doctors, the girls themselves), in what circumstances and for whose benefit, which dramatized the problems thrown up by the absence of commonly accepted norms. Do parents always know best? Are young women under the age of 16 capable of making rational decisions about something so emotive as sex and child-bearing? Is the universal availability of birth control advice and sex education an encouragement to promiscuity or the only rational protection against its consequences? The Guttmacher Institute which looked at the incidence of teenage pregnancy in several countries, found that the highest incidence was in the USA (96 pregnancies per 1,000 girls aged 15–19), the lowest in the Netherlands (14 per 1,000) with England and Wales somewhere in between (45 per 1,000) [7]. The conclusion was irresistible: that those countries with the greater availability of birth control and fairly comprhensive sex educations programmes have far lower pregnancy rates among teenagers. But information such as this does not still the argument: it merely dramatizes the radically different views that exist about the place and role of sex in our lives. Is sex for pleasure or procreation; should it be seen as a right or a privilege; is it an area of choice or of duty; does it have the same meaning for men and women? And when are we fit to be able to say yes or no? In the USA the question of sex education in schools became a battlefield because it symbolized the problems posed by sexual change. To liberals, sex education was the only means of spreading the information on which rational choices could be made. For conseratives, it threatened to undermine the family and open the road further to the secularization and demystification of sex. There appears to be little common ground between these tendencies.

All these changes have contributed to a third one: a change in the pattern of relationships which has led many to see a 'crisis of the family'. This perceived crisis has been traced to many roots and given various forms, but its focus has been an anxiety for the future of marriage, traditionally the privileged gateway to social status and sexual activity. After an increasing rate of marriage in the 1950s and early 1960s, a period when a higher percentage of men and women got married than ever before, a decline set in — in Sweden and Denmark from the mid-1960s, spreading to Britain, the USA and West Germany in the early 1970s, and France a little later. This was accompanied by a rise in cohabitation and a steep increase in the incidence of divorce. By the early 1980s something like a third of marriages looked set to end in divorce. In practice, fears of a collapse of marriage and the family proved somewhat premature. Except in Sweden, where cohabitation had a marriage-like stability, most cohabitees eventually married, and by the mid-1980s the marriage rate itself had bounced back, suggesting that what had happened was general deferment of marriage rather than its abandonment. And if one-third of marriages promised to end in divorce (a figure which itself showed signs of faltering by the mid-1980s) two-thirds would still survive. Moreover, up to 70 per cent of the divorced re-marry. Some sociologists saw signs in such figures not of the collapse of the traditional family, but of its re-emergence on new lines — the 'neo-conventional family' in the phrase of Robert Chester [8]: smaller than the Victorian family, with fewer children, possibly more equal in the distribution of domestic tasks, more prone perhaps to a pattern of 'serial monogamy' than in the past where marriage was, ideologically at least, for life.

But it was still very recognizably 'a family'. Most people are still born into a family, most dwell most of their lives in one, and most people still aspire to found one.

All this is true, and very important for assessing our material and sexual culture. At the same time it is equally vital to recognize a growing diversity of domestic forms, cutting across the apparent solidity of the conventional family. Within the broad limits of the term 'family itself there are many internal differences arising from different class, religious, racial, ethnic and political beliefs and practices. Alongside these different forms are various non-traditional patterns: never-married singlehood, non-marital cohabitation, voluntary childessness, 'the stepfamily' based on remarriage and the intermingling of children of different parents, single parenthood (within which term we must include both single-parent families created by divorce or death, and those created voluntarily, whether through conventional heterosexual intercourse or artifical insemination), so-called 'open marriages', multi-adult households, gay and lesbian couples — and probably many more [9].

Diversity is a growing fact but we have not yet adapted to it either in ideology or social policy. Our culture is suffused by familial values, to the extent that the language of family still provides the only vocabulary of truly lasting relatedness that we have. The result of this is very curious and paradoxical. On the one hand there are many who bemoan the decline of 'the traditional family' and all that was associated with that. On the other, for the many who do not live in a conventional relationship, the ideology of the family still dominates to the extent that there is no real alternative legitimation to that of the family itself, no other way for expressing our need for relationships. The traditional connection between marriage, the family and sexuality has been in part severed; but in its place we have no obvious single alternative — rather a plurality of forms. For many this diversity is a challenge; for others it represents a grave danger.

These changes in themselves, while important, have not transformed the sexual scene beyond recognition. Claims either of 'sexual liberation' or of 'moral decline' would seem to be wide of the mark. The complex intermingling of some very real changes has, however, caused a crisis of values and of meanings, a climate of uncertainty and (for some) confusion. In such a climate deep currents of feeling come to the surface and find expression in what are called moral panics. Moral panics are flurries of social anxiety, usually focusing on a condition or person, or group of persons, who become defined as a threat to accepted social values and assumptions. They arise generally in situations of confusion and ambiguity, in periods when the boundaries between legitimate and illegitimate behaviour seem to need redefining or classification. Classic moral panics in the past have often produced drastic results, in the form of moral witch-hunts, physical assault and legislative action. Since the Second World War there have been an apparently endless series, many of them focusing on moral and sexual issues: over venereal disease, prostitution, homosexuality, child sex abuse and paedophilia, teenage sex, pornography, 'video nasties' and so on. A significant feature in many of them has been the connection that has been made between sex and disease, disease becoming a metaphor for dirt, disorder and decay. Not surprisingly, recent panics have emerged over the social and moral connotations of genital herpes, cervical cancer and most recently and dramatically of all, AIDS (Acquired Immune Deficiency Syndrome). The impact of AIDS illustrates all the characteristic signs of a classic panic. More important for our discussion here, it reveals also the wider anxieties abroad about the current place of sexuality in our society. For this reason, the resulting crisis demands more than a passing glance. It throws light on many dark corners of our sexual culture, condensing a number of social stresses into a recognizable symbolic target [10].

One of the most striking features of the AIDS crisis is that, unlike most illnesses, from the first its chief victims were chiefly blamed for causing the disease, whether because of their social attitudes or sexual practices. And as most people suffering from the disease in Western countries were male homosexuals, this must tell us something about current attitudes and feelings towards unorthodox sexualities. From the earliest identification of the disease in America in 1981–82, AIDS was addressed as if it were a peculiarly homosexual affliction, and the term 'gay plague' became the common description of it in the more scabrous parts of the media. In fact it was clear from the beginning that other groups of people were prone to the disease: Haitians (in the USA) and intravenous drug abusers, and haemophiliacs, because of their dependence on other people's blood. It soon became apparent, too, that in large parts of central Africa, where the disease may have originated, and where it seemed to be endemic, it was the heterosexual population that was chiefly afflicted and it was therefore clearly transmittable through heterosexual intercourse. But it was the apparent connection between unorthodox sexual activity and the disease that chiefly fuelled the major elements of panic in the industrialized West.

In the normal course of a moral panic there is a characteristic stereotyping of the main actors as peculiar types of monsters, leading to an escalating level of fear and perceived threat, the taking up of panic stations and absolutist positions, and a search for symbolic, and usually imaginary solutions to the dramatized problem. In the case of AIDS there was a genuinely appalling disease, which devastated the lives of many people, for which there was no cure, and which at first seemed unstoppable in its rate of spread. By mid-1985 it had become the largest single cause of adult male deaths in New York City and was widespread elsewhere. Anxiety was legitimate. However, the form that the anxiety took was a search for scapegoats, and here gay men were peculiarly vulnerable. Certain sexual practices (for example anal intercourse) and social habits (multiple partners) generally (though often misleadingly) associated with male homosexuals were given a prime role in the spread of the disease, and it became easy to attribute blame to people with AIDS. From this a slippage readily took place: between the idea that homosexuals *caused* 'the plague' (itself without any backing in evidence) to the idea that homosexuality itself was a plague. A delegate at the Labour Party conference in Britain in 1985, opposing a motion in favour of gay and lesbian rights, incoherently summed up this confusion of views: 'This is an illness and sickness in our society and, because of this particular act — this unnatural act — we have this spreading disease of AIDS spreading throughout the world' [11]. Manifestations of what Susan Sontag has called 'practices of decontamination' [12], against women who were not vulnerable to it as well as men who were, soon appeared: restaurants refused to serve gay customers, gay waiters were sacked, dentists refused to examine the teeth of homosexuals, rubbish collectors wore masks when collecting garbage from suspected victims, prison officers refused to move prisoners, backstage staff in theatres refused to work with gay actors, distinguished pathologists refused to examine the bodies of AIDS patients, and undertakers refused to bury them.

The scientific evidence by mid-1985 was clear: AIDS was carried by a virus, which was not in itself exceptionally infectious. It was only possible to catch it through intimate sexual contact or interchange of blood. It was not a peculiarly homosexual disease, and most people in the world with the disease were in fact heterosexual. Moreover, its spread could, in all likelihood, be hindered by relatively small changes in lifestyle, particularly the avoidance of certain sexual practices (such as anal intercourse without protection).

All this suggested that what was needed was a public education campaign which both allayed fears and promoted an awareness of safer sexual activities. In places like California, New York, the Netherlands and other countries with traditionally liberal sexual regimes, this is what happened. Elsewhere, the response of governments was muted, and the interventions of moral conservatives fervent. In parts of North America and Australia there were calls for the segregation and confinement of those identified as having AIDS or potentially carrying it, bringing to memory the favoured solution to syphilis in the Britain of the 1860s: the compulsory examination and treatment of prostitutes suspected of disease under the provisions of the notorious Contagious Diseases Acts. In Britain a New Right commentator, responding to denunciations of the moral panic around AIDS, suggested that what was wanted was 'a little *more* moral panic' — against those who would argue that homosexuality was as normal as heterosexuality, and who would proselytize for it [13].

So what does this response tell us about contemporary attitudes? Susan Sontag has described the use of disease as a metaphor, with illness given a particular stigma when attached to groups or activities otherwise disapproved of [14]. Those who were first identified as being vulnerable to AIDS in the USA — Haitians and male homosexuals particularly — were all still on the margins of acceptability, whether because of a hidden agenda of racism or because of the continued social hostility to homosexuality. Both groups dramatize the changes that have overtaken what for many had once seemed a socially and morally integrated society. Homosexuality, in particular, as one of 'the perversions' which breached the expectations of orthodox behaviour, posed a threat for many to the traditional integration of sex, domesticity, social order and economic distribution enshrined in marriage and the family. It thus easily becomes a target for those alarmed by, and fearful of, change.

Beyond this there is a more elusive but equally powerful set of beliefs, those connecting sins and diseases in our imagination and fears. Disease sanctions still largely frame and organize many of our deepest sexual beliefs ('sick' is after all one of our favoured terms of abuse). It thus becomes easy for certain diseases which are connected, however tangentially in some cases, with sex, such as herpes, cervical cancer or AIDS, to appear as punishments, a divine retribution or nature's punishment for sexual misdemeanours. The term 'plague' itself, according to the *Oxford English Dictionary,* suggests this meaning. 'The poor homosexuals', said Patrick J. Buchanan, adviser to Presidents Nixon and Reagan, 'they have declared war upon nature, and now nature is exacting an awful retribution'. John Junor, editor of the (London) *Sunday Express* saw it rather less metaphysically, if not less moralistically:

If AIDS is not an Act of God with consequences just as frightful as fire and brimstone, then just what the hell is it? [15]

Secularization, liberalization, a change in the patterns of relationships, have all occurred, though with uneven effects. But they have left a deep residue of anxiety and guilt, of fear and loathing, which can as easily lead to a revival of moral absolutism as to further change.

REGULATING SEXUALITY

The crisis of sexual meanings has accentuated the problem of how to regulate and control sexuality. What we believe sex is, or ought to be, structures our responses to it. So it is difficult to separate the particular meanings we give to sex from the forms of control we advocate. If we regard sex as dangerous, disruptive and fundamentally antisocial, then we are likely to embrace moral and political positions which propose tight, authoritarian regulation. This I shall call the absolutist position. If, on the other hand, we believe that the powers of desire are basically benign, life-enhancing and liberating we are liable to adopt a relaxed, even radical set of values, to support a libertarian stance. Somewhere between these two extreme positions we will find a third: it is perhaps rather less certain about whether sex in itself is good or bad; it is convinced, however, of the evils both of moral authoritarianism and of excess. This I shall call the liberal or liberal-pluralist position. These three approaches — or strategies of regulation — have all been present in our culture for a long time. They still largely provide the framework — whether consciously or subliminally — for current debates about sex and politics.

Historically, we are heirs of the absolutist tradition. This has been based on a fundamental belief that the disruptive powers of sex can only be controlled by a clear-cut morality, intricately embedded in a particular set of social institutions: marriage, heterosexuality, family life and (at least in the Judaic–Christian traditions), monogamy. This absolutist morality is deeply rooted in the Christian West, but though its grounding may be in religion, it is today a much wider cultural and political phenomenon, embraced as readily by the atheist as by the Christian (or other religious) who is ready to worship at the foot of strong, moral values. Moral absolutism has deeply influenced our general culture, and in particular the forms of legal regulation, many of which still survive. The major set of legal changes in Britain in the last decades of the nineteenth century and the early part of this century (on obscenity, prostitution, age of consent, homosexuality, incest) were pushed for by absolutist social morality movements, propelled in many cases by a religious fervour, and frequently in alliance with moral feminism. Though tempered by selective enforcement and pragmatic adjustments (for example on prostitution, where moralistic censure and tacit acceptance lived side by side), these laws continued to define sexual offences until the 1960s, and sometimes beyond.

Like the absolutist approach, the libertarian tradition embraces various strands of belief. One important element has a surprising affinity, in its fundamental assumptions about what sex is, to moral absolutism. A major literary tradition, from the Marquis de Sade through the 'decadents' of the late nineteenth century to more or less contemporary writers such as George Bataille and Jean Genet, celebrate sex as danger and transgression. Like the Christian absolutists they appear to see sexuality as threatening the self, the society and even the universe. Unlike the absolutists they believe it should [16]. Transgressive sex is a way of breaking out of the tyranny of the existing order. Here they join with the other libertarian strand, who similarly believe that sexual liberation is a (perhaps *the*) key to social freedom, a disruptive energy that can help break the existing order. The difference is that these libertarians believe that sex is fundamentally good and healthy, a force blocked only by the power of 'civilization' or capitalism. There is often here a close affinity with a strong socialist tradition, stretching from pioneers like Charles Fourier and Edward Carpenter to Wilhelm Reich in the 1930s and Herbert Marcuse in the 1950s and 1960s. Such a political libertarianism had enormous influence in the developing sexual politics of the late 1960s. The problem with the absolutist and libertarian traditions is that they both take for granted fundamentally essentialist views about what sex is. Sexuality in itself appears not only as a powerful energy which is outside and opposed to society, but also, because of this, a natural force which appears to embody its own morality. Values and theoretical assumptions about the nature of sex are closely related. In this sense, libertarianism and absolutism are mirror-images of one another: both are committed to a view of sexuality which transcends the bounds of mere history.

In practice, however, the regulation of sexuality for the past generation has been dominated by varying forms of the liberal tradition. I say 'varying forms' because there are considerable shifts of interpretation between one culture and another, with different emphases particularly apparent between North America and Europe. In the United States the central organizing idea is that of 'rights': it is significant, for example, that in the debates over abortion each side uses the language of fundamental rights, the rights of the unborn child versus the rights of the mother to control over her body. As this illustrates, to speak of rights does not end the discussion. We are still left with the problem of which person's rights are paramount in what specific situation, and whose rights are taken up can often be a clearly political rather than an *a priori* moral issue. In the case of abortion there are conflicting values at play. The result is a battle between rival absolutes in which each side has only its own passion and ability to mobilize support to rely on.

In Britain, on the other hand, the idea of fundamental civil rights is not enshrined either in a written constitution, a bill of rights, or in clear-out legislation. The liberal tradition is, nevertheless, very deeply entrenched, and in relationship to sexuality is has been very clearly and influentially articulated — most famously in the Wolfenden Committee report on prostitution and male homosexuality, published in 1957 [17]. The point of confluence with the American tradition is in the emphasis both approaches put on achieving an appropriate balance between private and public spheres. The Wolfenden report made the distinction classically clear. It was, it proposed, the duty of the law to regulate the public sphere, and in particular to maintain public decency. There were limits, however, in its obligation to control the private sphere, the traditional arena of personal morality. Churches might strive to tell people what to do in their private lives. It was not the task of the state to attempt to do the same. The state, therefore, had no place in the enforcement of private standards. In such an approach there was a tacit acceptance that society was no longer — if it ever had been — governed by a moral consensus, and that there was in practice a plurality of alternative moral views abroad. The law should therefore limit its role to the maintenance of common standards of public decency.

The 'Wolfenden strategy' provided the theoretical framework for the series of reforms concerning sexuality that were enacted in Britain in the 1960s: reforms in the laws on obscenity, homosexuality, abortion, theatre censorship and divorce [18]. Their starting point was the belief that absolutist approaches were inadequate for regulating sexuality, because there was no common morality to underpin them. It was striking that most of the leading Christian Churches, especially those closely related to the established order like the Church of England, endorsed this assumption: they may not have approved of homosexuality, abortion or divorce, but they clearly believed that they could no longer expect the law itself to enshrine this moral position.

There was more than a simple moral agnosticism in this rationalized approach. There was also an implicit feeling that the law itself was no longer, if it had ever been, an appropriate or effective means for attempting to control private sexual behaviour. There was a search in many of the debates around sexuality in the period for alternative methods of regulation, which concentrated on limiting harm rather than eliminating sin. Havelock Ellis had already articulated the characteristic approach in the 1930s:

The question is no longer: Is the act abnormal? It becomes: Is the act injurious? [19]

The Wolfenden report itself discussed whether homosexuality and prostitution could be regarded as sicknesses, best treated by medicine rather than law. It concluded that they were not diseases but nevertheless advocated further research into their 'aetiologies' (origins and development), and one of the assumptions of the reformers who followed was that medicine or welfare agencies were better placed than the legal authorities to properly regulate sexuality: it was doctors in the abortion reform law of 1967 who were given the prime responsibility for deciding whether a woman should or should not be allowed termination of their pregnancies, not the woman herself.

The reforms conformed, then, to a liberal strategy which limited direct interference in private lives. But they did not necessarily abandon the idea of control — the law was actually tightened in relationship to *public* displays of prostitution and homosexuality — nor did they positively enshrine new rights. There was no abortion on demand, no legally enshrined right to divorce by mutual consent, and male homosexuality was not fully legalized: certain types of homosexual behaviour, between consenting adults (over 21) in private, were decriminalized but not legitimized, and this was representative. Just as the liberal approach was agnostic on the effectiveness of the law in a complex society, so it was agnostic about the merits of the activities it directed its attention towards.

The reforms of the 1960s were of great importance and they certainly provided the preconditions for many of the changes of the 1970s. Some of the results were spectacular. Between 1968 and 1980 over a million legal abortions had been carried out. The divorce rate trebled for those under 25 between 1970 and 1979, and doubled for those over 25. New possibilities opened up for discussing sex, in books and the theatre, and for developing new lifestyles. But changes did not all go in one direction. At the same time as male homosexuality was decriminalized, which for the first time made possible a publicly affirmed homosexual way of life, between 1967 and 1976 the recorded incidents of indecency between men doubled, the number of prosecutions trebled and the number of convictions quadrupled. Several attempts were made to limit abortions. The divorce legislation led to agitated efforts to come to terms with the child-care and financial consequences. This illustrates what Stuart Hall has called 'the double taxonomy' of freedom *and* control that lay behind the reforms, and they scarcely justified Mary Whithouse's forecasts that the reforms had produced a 'progressive moral disarmament of the nation by law' [20], with worse to come.

Nevertheless, the reforms themselves became symbolic of all the other changes that were taking place, and the sticking point for those who wanted to halt the tide of liberalism and permissiveness. In the USA where, true to tradition, reforms had been achieved through court action rather than law changes, the key decision of the Supreme Court in 1973 to allow abortion became the occasion for what has been described as a 'moral civil war' between contending forces [21]. In Britain the 1960s reforms became the target for vigorous attempts at restrictive amendment, and, even more critically, set targets for conservative counter-attacks.

One of the difficulties of the liberal strategy in out-facing these challenges was that, while it certainly disturbed conservative moralists, the approach did not, on the whole engage the energetic support of radical forces, largely because of its hesitant or narrow endorsement of sexual pluralism. Moreover, the approach itself had severe weaknesses when faced with the growing complexities of sex-related questions in the face of rapid change. The confused response to the report of the committee on obscenity and film censorship, chaired by Bernard Williams in the late 1970s, illustrates the problem. In its attempt to delineate a response to sexually explicit material which would accord with generally accepted standards, it not only offended the right but failed to engage any enthusiastic support from liberals and feminists [22]. The difficulties of the Wolfenden strategy were even more strikingly illustrated by the reaction to the new reproductive technologies in the early 1980s: the problems posed, in particular, by artificial insemination by donor (AID), by *in vitro* fertilization (IVF) and the use of surrogate mothers, and by embryological research. The report of the Warnock Committee on human fertilization and embryology, in grappling with these issues, observed that there were two levels to the debate [23]. The first was the issue of whether there could be general agreement that an action was right or wrong in itself (for example, surrogacy or AID). The second was still the more difficult problem that, even if there was unanimity over a particular activity, would it be justified to intervene to enforce a moral view? On the question, say, of research using human embryos, the classic liberal distinctions between private pleasure and public policy could not operate. The desire for positive results from embryological research might be a private goal (encouraged by the hope, for example, of finding a clue to certain genetically transmitted illnesses) but it was likely to be publicly financed, and therefore the subject of political decisions. At the same time it raised appallingly difficult ethical questions about the nature of life and the obligations of science.

In a case such as this the provision of a formal framework for separating the law and private morality could not in itself be a satisfactory method for dealing with difficult questions of choice or conflicts of values. Not surprisingly, questions of how embryological research should be controlled, and about the merits of commercial surrogacy, became immediate political controversies cutting across conventional party divisions and transcending traditional liberal alliances. This illustrates again that politics, morality and sexuality do not inhabit separate spheres of social life. They are intimately and inextricably connected in the actual political and social climate in which we live.

THE POLITICS OF SEXUALITY

The possibilities of political mobilization around sexual matters have been greatly enhanced by the significant shifts in the social and cultural configuration of the industrialized countries in the past twenty years. Rapid economic growth followed by slump, the dissolution of old class boundaries and the reconstruction of new, the rise and partial decline of welfarism, important changes in the relationship between the sexes, within the family and local communities — in short the changing social geography of the Western countries — have produced new social tensions and antagonisms, forms of domination and resistance, that have shaken traditional political forms and methods. The new antagonisms and resulting social movements have not displaced the old ones, of class, race, ethnicity, or gender; in many ways struggles around these issues have been reinvigorated during the past generation, and have been closely linked with one another. The American black movement in the 1960s was not only critically important in asserting the claims of the racially oppressed to justice; it also provided an organizational stimulus to the revival of the women's movement, while at the same time raising questions about different family patterns and the racist organization of sexualities. But alongside these more traditionally recognizable forms of resistance, new ones have arisen — for peace, the environment, and most relevant for our purposes here, around sexual preferences and choices.

Feminism and the gay and lesbian movements in all the major Western countries — but above all in the USA — have transformed the traditional debates on sex by asserting a new claim to self-definition and self-determination on all issues concerning the body and its pleasures. These new social–sexual movements have created, in effect, an alternative public sphere of personal interaction, debate, publications and intellectual concourse, creating in the process what amounts to a 'grass roots sexology' which has challenged the certainties of the sexual tradition. The radical movements concerned with sexuality are by no means unified or coherent in either their means or ends. They have, however, introduced a new element into contemporary politics, constructing new 'communities of interest', new constituencies and a new moral agenda. The result has been a major expansion in the meaning of the term of 'politics', to embrace not only new movements but also a new range of concerns — with what seemed hitherto microscopically personal issues, concerning health, the body, values, choices and pleasures.

This new politics of sexuality may have created new spaces. It has also, however, opened new fissures and generated new hostilities. There is no doubt that one of the contributions to the rise of the 'New Right' in America, with its own moral agenda, was deep hostility to what was seen as the moral and social collapse represented by feminism and lesbian and gay politics. Alongside potently emotive issues such as national decline, racial conflict, bureaucratic welfarism and economic change, defence of 'the family', and the idea of traditional moral and sexual values encoded in that term, became a powerful rallying point for those disrupted by change and fearful of the future. The New Right, in looking for issues that people cared about, found that social issues, fitted the bill [24]. The question is: why do people care so much about these issues? The answer seems to lie, in part at least, in the crucial importance we attach to boundary maintenance in staving off challenges to social status and sexual identity. The new sexual politics since the 1960s has deeply unsettled existing boundaries, in questioning the fixity of male and female attributes, the divide between adults and children, the relationship between procreation and sex, between the genitals and sexual pleasure, and many other issues. They have thrown into the melting pot many taken-for-granted beliefs, and caused confusion in the mental universe of many people, especially those already threatened by other changes. In such situations some react with violence, and with demands for moral segregation, retribution, and the re-establishment of the old (if largely mythical) disciplines.

The key to the paradox of sexual politics during the 1980s is that, while it was generally left-inclined radical social movements that raised new questions about sexuality, it was the right that proved best able to utilize the energies and forces aroused to weld together an effective political force. This was especially true in the USA, where the 'Moral Majority' became an important adjunct to the new conservative alliances that brought President Reagan to power. The value of the 'social issues' was that they provided an ideological framework to construct and effectively organize a potentially powerful mass base for conservative politics, to articulate social anxiety through focusing on a symbolic enemy, in which sexual liberalism, 'permissiveness', 'sexual anarchy' (the phrases varied) became an explanation for social ills. In the USA this new moral politics was able to call on a potentially wide constituency of support — a resurgent fundamentalism in religion amongst Catholics, born-again Protestants, Mormons and militant Jews, a disaffected small town constituency, women disturbed by the threat posed by feminism, and many others. It was able to deploy its support effectively because of a new and more fluid political situation associated with the decline of the old party machines and the increasing power of single-issue campaigns. Increasingly, instrumental politics in America seemed on the road to being displaced by symbolic issues [25]. This was much less true of other major industrialized countries, where traditional political boundaries and social divisions around class seemed more entrenched. But even in Britain, defence of the family proved an important, if secondary, element of the appeal represented by Margaret Thatcher and her Conservatives in the general elections of 1979 and 1983, while the restoration of social discipline and law and order became a central *motif* in her bid for re-election for a third term. Moral issues can mobilize people.

The success of this conservative sexual politics has been variable. There is plentiful evidence that it has not fundamentally shifted public opinion anywhere in the West, which on issues such as abortion remains apparently liberal. Even on homosexuality public opinion has become considerably more tolerant than it was in that era of permissiveness, the 1960s. Nevertheless, it has had significant effects in political terms because of its influence in government circles, and has been able in the USA to shift the focus of public policy on abortion, sex education and pornography, as well as the general tenor of debate. The appointment by the Reagan administration of conservative judges to the higher courts means that, in a political culture where legal processes are a critical element in the shaping of public policy, the moral agenda for the 1990s is likely to be set by New Right attitudes of the 1980s.

But perhaps the most potent effect of this more confident moral politics is that it has tended to reveal the divisions and incoherences of more clearly radical social movements. The debate over pornography is particularly illuminating here. For moral conservatives pornography has been the most obvious symbol of what has gone wrong, revealing most graphically the separation of sex and moral values. For feminists, too, it has been a crucial issue, above all because it vividly represents the sexual exploitation of women, throwing a strong searchlight into the heart of male power. Some feminists, however, have gone further, and see pornography as not only representative of violence but actually *as* violence against women, and therefore the critical enemy of feminist aspiration. The result in America and elsewhere has been a tacit alliance between some feminists and moral conservatives in legal attempts to ban pornography [26]. Their starting points might be different, as are their ultimate goals. Nevertheless the alliance means a blurring of the edges of differing campaigns, and many see this ostensibly tactical move by some feminists as a fundamental abandonment of radical sexual politics.

This is an aspect of a wider debate about the place of sexual politics in contemporary politics that has been particularly stimulated by modern feminism. A potential division has been observed between on the one hand a 'politics of sexism' and on the other a 'politics of desire' [27]. The first, the domain of classical 'sexual politics', has been preoccupied above all with the reality of female subordination — economic, social and sexual. During the 1970s there was an increasing stress on the power of the existing male dominated sexual codes — particularly 'compulsory heterosexuality' — in perpetuating female oppression. This stress offered a valuable antidote to the politics which ignored sexuality or saw it as secondary to other issues. It led to a new concentration on questions such as sexual violence, rape, sexual exploitation of children, pornography and the political nature of lesbianism which have been genuinely important. But it also led to a new emphasis on the differences between male and female sexualities, and upon women as victims of male power and desire. Alice Echols has commented:

as recent feminism has become synonymous with the reclamation of and establishment of a so-called female principle, it has come to reflect and reproduce dominant assumptions about women. [28]

That is, it is in complicity with conventional beliefs in male aggression and female passivity. It is in opposition to this that a 'politics of desire' has emerged more vocally amongst feminists. This does not dismiss the import-ance of the issues raised by debates about violence and exploitation. It seeks to stress, however, the positive possibilities of sexual freedom, questions of pleasure as well as power, of choice as well as victimization.

The polarity between these two tendencies is in some ways misleading. Those who concentrate on women's victimization have their own vision of sexual fulfilment, just as the proponents of a politics of desire are aware of the strengths of the structures of dominance and subordination over women. Nevertheless, the difference of emphasis between these two strands raised vital issues, which exploded in the late 1970s and early 1980s into major divisions between feminists as they took up polarized positions around topics like sado-masochism, homosexuality and pornography [29]. This in turn is an aspect of a wider dilemma amongst liberals and leftists during the 1980s about how best to respond to the sexual crisis. There appeared to be a general belief that there was much that was wrong or inadequate about the changes of the previous generation. Sexual freedom for men might actually have increased the sexual subordination of women. At the same time, there was a growing awareness that much that had been inherited from a more authoritarian past had not really changed: laws and social conventions still limited sexual choice, in everything from sexual preference and reproductive rights to the free distribution of reading materials and visual representation.

At the heart of the dilemma was the question of how best to respond to the ever-growing reality of sexual diversity. In attempting to work through this issue, in all its delicacy and complexity, it became clear to many that politics, values, and ethics are not separate spheres. They are inextricably linked in the modern politics of sexuality.

REFERENCES

[1] Alfred C. Kinsey, Wardell P. Pomeroy and Clyde E. Martin, *Sexual Behavior in the Human Male,* W. B. Saunders, Philadelphia and London (1948), p. 21.

[2] Dennis Altman, 'Sex: the new front line for gay politics', *Socialist Review,* No. 6, Sept.–Oct. 1982.

[3] Speech of 27 March 1982.

[4] Ronald Butt, 'Lloyd George knew his followers', *The Times* (London), 19 September 1985.

[5] Quoted in Michael Tracey and David Morrison, *Whitehouse,* Macmillan, London (1979), p. 177.

[6] See the discussion of these tendencies in Jeffrey Weeks, *Sex, Politics and Society. The Regulation of Sexuality Since 1800,* Longman, Harlow (1981), Chapter 13; and *Sexuality and its Discontents. Meanings, Myths and Modern Sexualities,* Rowtledge & Kegan Paul, London (1985), Chapter 2.

[7] Quoted in Virginia Ironside, 'How Mrs Gillick has hijacked morality', in *The Guardian* (London), 23 July 1985. For a discussion of teenage sex see Judith Bury, *Teenage Pregnancy in Britain,* Birth Control Trust, London (1984).

[8] Robert Chester, 'The rise of the neo-conventional family', *New Society,* 9 May 1985.

[9] See, for example, Eleanor D. Macklin, 'Non-traditional family forms: a decade of research', *Journal of Marriage and the Family,* **42,** 1980, pp. 905–922; and the essays in R. N. Rapaport *et al., Families in Britain,* Routledge & Kegan Paul, London (1982).

[10] For a full discussion see Dennis Altman, *AIDS and the Mind of America,* Doubleday, New York (1986), published in Britain as *AIDS and the New Puritans,* Pluto, London (1986). See also my comments in *Sexuality and its Discontents,* pp. 44–53.

[11] Quoted in *Daily Telegraph* (London), 5 October 1985.

[12] Susan Sontag, *Illness as Metaphor,* Penguin, Harmondsworth (1983).

[13] Digby Anderson, 'No moral panic — that's the problem', *The Times* (London, 18 June 1985.

[14] Sontag, op.cit.

[15] *New York Post,* 24 May 1983; *Sunday Express,* 24 February 1985.

[16] This 'gnostic' approach is discussed in Muray S. Davis, *Smut: Erotic Reality/Obscene Ideology,* University of Chicago Press, Chicago and London (1983).

[17] Home Office, Scottish Home Department, *Report of the Committee on Homosexual Offences and Prostitution,* Cmnd 247, Her Majesty's Stationary Office, London (1957).

[18] On these see my *Sex, Politics and Society,* Chapter 13.

[19] Ellis, *The Psychology of Sex,* William Heinemann, London (1946; first published 1933), p. 183.

[20] Stuart Hall, 'Reformism and the legislation of consent', in National Deviancy Conference (ed.), *Permissiveness and Control. The Fate of the Sixties Legislation,* Macmillan, London (1980); Tracey and Morrison, *Whitehouse,* p. 67.

[21] Malcolm Potts, 'America's battle over abortion', *New Society,* 7 February 1985.

[22] Home Office, *Report of the Committee on Obscenity and Film Censorship,* Cmnd 7772, Her Majesty's Stationery Office, London (1979).

[23] Mary Warnock, *A Question of Life. The Warnock Report on Human Fertilisation and Embryology,* Basil Blackwell, Oxford (1985).

[24] See, 'The New Right: a special report', *Conservative Digest,* June 1979.

[25] See the discussion in Jerry G. Pankhurst and Sharon K. Houseknecht, 'The family, politics and religion in the 1980s', *Journal of Family Issues,* **4,** 1983, pp. 5–34.

[26] See, for example, 'The war against pornography', *Newsweek,* 18 March 1985, pp. 58–67.

[27] Kenneth Plummer, 'Sexual diversity: a sociological perspective', in K. Howells (ed.), *Sexual Diversity,* Blackwell, Oxford (1984).

[28] Alice Echols, 'The new feminism of yin and yang', in Ann Snitow, Christine Stansell and Sharon Thompson (eds.), *Desire: The Politics of Sexuality,* Virago, London (1985), p. 62.

[29] Carole Vance discusses these in her chapter in Vance (ed.), *Pleasure and Danger. Exploring Female Sexuality,* Routledge & Kegan Paul, Boston and London (1984). See also Weeks, *Sexuality and its Discontents,* Chapter 9.

6

Private pleasures and public policy

> If human nature is historical, individuals have different histories and
> therefore different needs
>
> Michael Ignatieff [1]

There are many questions we could ask about sexuality: about duty and obligation, morality and immorality, goodness and evil, health and sickness, truth and falsity. Subtle, and not so subtle, debates around some or all of these dichotomies have dominated the Western discourse on sexuality for over two thousand years. Whatever the range of answers that may be reached, they all have the distinction of carrying a heavy weight of prescription, of telling people, often very coercively, how they must behave in order to attain the good (or moral or hygienic) life. The unifying thread of this essay, however, is that the idea of sexuality has been loaded down with too many assumptions, that it has lumbered under a weight of expectations it cannot, and should not have to, bear. 'Sex acts', Gayle Rubin has rightly said, 'are burdened with an excess of significance' [2]. We should lighten the load.

One of the major difficulties in doing this has been the privileged role claimed by the experts on sex over the past hundred years in telling us what is good or bad, appropriate or inappropriate behaviour. In his Presidential address to the 1929 Congress of the World League for Sexual Reform, Magnus Hirschfeld declared that: 'A sexual ethics based on science is the only sound system of ethics' [3]. The impulse behind this statement was noble indeed. Hirschfeld like other luminaries of this first phase of the sexological revolution, looked forward to a new enlightment in which prejudice, religious moralism, and authoritarian sexual codes would dissolve before the light of reason as provided by the new science of sex.

Sexual knowledge and sexual politics marched hand in hand as the sexologists, like Hirschfeld, Havelock Ellis and Auguste Forel (joint Presidents of the World League in 1929) also became the patrons of sex reform, while sexual reformers of various hues, from feminist birth controllers to campaigners for homosexual rights, looked to the scientists for guidelines to further their activities. 'Through science to Justice', Hirschfeld famously proclaimed as the watchword of his Scientific–Humanitarian Committee. It was the motto of the whole sex reform movement. The problem then, as now, was that the insights of this new science were not straightforward or unequivocal: to put it bluntly, sexologists disagreed with one another. Homosexual activists might look to Hirschfeld's theories which said that they belonged to a biologically given 'third' or 'intermediate' sex to justify their claims to social justice, but the Nazis who burned Hirschfeld's library and legacy after 1933 could equally well use more or less the same arguments to disqualify homosexuals altogether, as biological anomalies, from the new moral order — and find scientists to support them. Sexologists might point out the fact that sexuality was a rich and varied continent, but they also lent their weight to normalizing institutions, to attempts at 'cures', and to eugenic solutions to the 'problems' of over population and the proliferation of the 'feeble-minded'. Havelock Ellis was not alone in being a sexual reformer, and also a supporter of the eugenic breeding of 'the best' (inevitably defined by class and racial criteria). The proliferating literature on married love might encourage the belief that women, too, were sexual beings deserving of satisfaction and pleasure. But these marriage experts also managed to pathologize the single woman and to sustain a burgeoning literature on the inadequacies of 'frigid' women.

The ultimate political and moral implications of sexual enlightenment were at best ambiguous and at worst dangerous as they contributed a scientific justification for essentially traditional or authoritarian positions. By the 1920s social purity organizations were looking to the writings of Ellis, Freud and others to underpin their modified but still fundamentally normalizing positions. Over the half century since, the science of sex has been drawn upon to justify a huge variety of moral positions, from passionate advocacy of sexual revolution to fervent endorsement of sexual orthodoxy. Today, even the least theoretical of moral entrepreneurs is able to call on an encyclopaedia of would-be-scientific arguments to sustain her or his position, from hormonal theories for explaining sexual difference and perversity to 'the silent whisperings' of sociobiology to justify the inevitability of inequality.

This is not a polemic aimed at the rejection of any attempt at a scientific understanding of the workings of the body or the mind. It is, however, an argument for abandoning the claim that sexology alone provides an objective guide into the truth of our bodies, and hence a code by which we should live our personal and social lives. The 'science of sex', like every other science, is enmeshed in the web of social relations. We should accordingly treat its more extravagant claims, especially when it is dealing with humans in all their contrariness, with caution and a sensitivity to their origins.

Against the sexual tradition which sexology has done so much to sustain I have sought in this essay to *problematize* the idea of sexuality, to show its emergence from an intricate history, its close implication in relations of power, its deployment to sustain and normalize certain forms of erotic activity and its marginalization of others, and the crisis of meanings that has resulted from the diverse challenges which it has produced. But we are still left with a question which looms ever larger as we contemplate the domain of sexuality: what should the place of sex be in our individual lives in the contemporary world? This is scarcely a minor question. At its heart is the old, old question of ethics, of how we should live [4].

The critique of essentialism which underpins this work has been very useful in casting light on hidden but controlling assumptions, and in opening up the sexual field to new questions, about history, power, meanings, diversity, choice and so on. It has, on the whole, been less successful in providing maps for navigating the highways and byways of what is still, despite all the torrents of writing about it, a partly uncharted country. The reason for this lack is quite straightforward. Sexology offered an alternative world outlook to the religious cosmology much of its initial energy was directed against. It claimed to be uncovering the truth of Nature in opposition to the truths of mere prejudice or tradition. But if scientific knowledge itself is suspect, what is left?

If we reject the hierarchy of sexual values laid down by the science of sex, how do we distinguish between the normal and the abnormal? If, as Foucault said with reference to Sade, 'sex is without any norm or intrinsic rule that might be formulated from its own nature' [5], how do we determine appropriate and inappropriate behaviour? If we can no longer regard sex as either intrinsically threatening and evil, or liberating and good, how can we escape the Scylla of moralism on the one hand and the Charybdis of anything-goes libertarianism on the other? Finally, if we can no longer accept the politics of the old 'sexual revolutionaries' because of their essentialism, and not believe in a transcendent 'sexual liberation', because of the inevitable involvement of sex in the intricate play of power, what are sexual politics for? Recent liberation movements, Foucault observed in a later interview, 'suffer from the fact that they cannot find any principle on which to base the elaboration of the new ethics . . . [other than] an ethics founded on so-called scientific knowledge of what the self is, what desire is, what the unconscious is, and so on' [6]. The trouble is that this 'scientific knowledge' is, as we know, full of divisions and contradictions about what the self is, what desire may be, and even whether there is such a thing as 'the unconscious'. Yet if we reject these guidelines, is there anything left?

Foucault's own late attempt to grapple with this dilemma, in the two volumes of his *History* published at the very end of his life, is characteristically indirect. The two volumes are superficially at least simple exegesies of ancient Greek and Latin texts on how people should live [7]. But their very indirection and lack of obvious contact with today's problems serves to clarify what is at stake. He likens the world of the Greeks and Romans to our own in one key respect. Like us post-Christians, they were faced with the task of elaborating an ethic that was not founded in religion or any other *a priori* justification, least of all science. Like us they were troubled with moral questions around what we term sexuality (the nearest equivalent for them was called *aphrodisia*). Many of the concerns have in fact been continuous for over 2,000 years: with the body, the relations of men and women, of men and men. Unlike us, however, they did not attempt a codification of acts which made sex itself the bearer of negative values and moral anxieties, nor attempt a subordination of individuals to external rules of conduct based on such values and anxieties. They sought instead an 'aesthetics of existence', an art of life in which temperance balanced excess, self-discipline kept pleasures in order.

They were preoccupied with methods of self-knowledge, with techniques of the self, rules of conduct organized around dietary matters (the individual's relation with his body), economics (the conduct of the head of the household) and the erotic (the relations of men and boys). They were, in other words, seeking modes of life which derived not from a central truth about sex, but from the set of relations in which the individual was embedded. The aim was to define the uses of pleasure in a way which neither ignored it, nor surrendered to its intoxicating force.

Foucault is not of course suggesting that this is a model for our own time. This was an ethics for 'free men', from which women, children and slaves were excluded. He rejects as a matter of principle the evocation of golden ages, and anyway the Ancient World was scarcely golden. But in a typically oblique manner, what he is doing in examining a time so different from our own is to throw our own needs and aspirations into relief. What we lack, he is suggesting, in not a transcendent truth, but ways of coping with a multiplicity of truths. We need not so much a morality based on absolute values, but an ethics (and politics I would add), for allowing us to cope with a variety of choices. Foucault, in taking us through the arts of existence in the ancient world, is asking us to reflect on the ways of life that could be valid for us today.

What would the basis of a modern sexual ethics be? There are hints in the distinction Foucault makes between freedom of 'sexual acts' and freedom of 'sexual choice'. He is against the first, he suggests, not least because it might involve endorsement of violent activity such as rape. It is also, of course, the mode of the sexual tradition. But he is for the second, whether it be, as he puts it 'the liberty to manifest that choice or not to manifest it' [8]. The tenor of this is that the nature of the social relationships in which choice becomes meaningful is of crucial importance. We are being urged to move away from a situation where we judge the nature of the act, to one where we consider the context and the meaning of the act for the participants. I have already suggested some of the implications of this in the chapter on diversity. Here I want to look at the wider implications, for it points away from an absolutist morality, based on a fundamental human nature, to a fully pluralistic ethic, based on the acceptance of diverse tastes.

I have described this approach elsewhere as 'radical pluralism': pluralistic because it starts off with an assumption of the *fact* of diverse tastes, pleasures, and relationships; radical because of the positive endorsement of variety as a necessary accompaniment of our increasingly complex world. Rubin has argued that despite all the very real changes that have occurred:

> This culture always treats sex with suspicion. It construes and judges any sexual practice in terms of its worst possible expression. Sex is presumed guilty until proven innocent. [9]

Moral pluralism begins with a different belief: that sex in itself is neither good nor bad; but is rather a field of possibilities and potentialities, all of which must be judged by the context in which they occur. It opens the way then, to acceptance of diversity as the *norm* of our culture and the appropriate means of thinking about sexuality.

This does not, of course, still all difficulties: in many ways, in fact, it compounds them. It is far easier to confront each difficult area of choice with a moral code which tells us exactly, and invariably, how we should live. In a social climate of rapid social — and moral — change, and of the emergence of new social possibilities, identities and lifestyles, it is a temptation to seek once again the security of absolute moral standards, which fixes us in a world of certainty where personal and social identities are given. Moral absolutism, as Alvin Gouldner has observed, 'serves to cut the Gordian knot of indecision' [10], magically sweeping away doubt and anxiety and making possible the onward march of the army of the just. The radical pluralist approach, in sharp distinction to the absolutist tradition, is tentative, provisional and open-ended. It can be seen as partaking of some of the elements of the libertarian tradition — especially what may be called its 'sex-positive' attitudes — while at the same time it shares with the liberal tradition a recognition of the need for careful distinctions, for a grasp of meaning and context, and of the importance of the discourse of rights and choice. Where it differs from both these traditions is in its decisive recognition of the social production of sexualities, and their complex embeddedness in diverse power relations. Its aim, consequently, is to provide guidelines for decision making rather than new absolute values. It rejects the temptation of a 'radical morality', whether one derived from the traditions of feminism or of socialism, two political discourses which lay particular claim to moral insight. Instead it places its emphasis on the merits of choice, and the conditions which limit choice.

Choice implies, in the first place, democracy. 'Democracy' may seem an odd word to apply to the sexual sphere, but it is surely a new concept of democracy that is called for when we speak of the right to control our bodies, when we say 'our bodies are our own'. The claim to bodily self-determination is an old one, with roots in a number of different moral and political traditions. From liberal roots in the puritan revolution of the seventeenth century we can trace the evolution of the idea of 'property in one's own person'. The Marxist tradition offers a vision of society in which human needs may be satisfied harmoniously. From the biological sciences comes the understanding of the body, its capacities and limitations, establishing the boundaries of individual possibility. All three of these recognize limits to the free exercise of bodily self-determination: through traditional, patriarchal authority, the unequal distribution of property and power, or the limits of the personality itself, with its needs for physical sustenance, emotional warmth, and above all, social involvement. From feminism has come a recognition of further limitations, the subtle coercions of a male-dominated society and the infiltration of inequality through all the relations of social life. Coward has argued:

> When we hear talk of freedom to choose sexual partners, we can be sure we'll also hear talk of visual appeal, the mysterious alchemy which strikes from the blue at the most awkward moments. And here's the coercion. Because women are compelled to make themselves attractive in certain ways, and those ways involve submitting to the culture's beliefs about appropriate

sexual behaviour, women's appearances are laden down with cultural values, and women have to form their identities within these values, or, with difficulty, against them. [11]

A 'democratic morality', it has been suggested would judge acts by the way partners deal with one another, the consideration they show for each other, the absence of coercion, the degree of pleasure and need they can satisfy [12]. These are admirable goals, but their recognition can be constantly thwarted by an awareness of the constraints that limit free choice.

There are real limitations in the society we live in to the free play of choice. But there is another issue which looms whenever the questions of choice is raised: where should choice end? Should people be free, for instance, to choose activities that may harm themselves or others, whether intentionally or not. The problem here is not so much one of physical harm — which can be measured — but of psychic or moral damage — which usually cannot. Should, say, a just society ban pornography because of its exploitative representations of women? Should sado-masochistic sex be tolerated even between, in the famous phrase, 'consenting adults in private'? Harm is, of course, a difficult word to start with. Havelock Ellis in the 1930s, in what was to become a classical liberal formulation of the issue, believed that it was such a difficult concept that condemnation or interference could only be called for in two cases: if the subjects were in danger of damaging their health, and therefore likely to call on medical or psychotherapeutic treatment; or if there was a danger of injury to the health or rights of others, in which case the law was entitled to interfere [13]. These are, on the surface at least, very sensible guidelines, but they ignore a factor that has assumed a growing importance in recent debates on sexuality, a belief that 'damage' or 'harm' can be moral as well as physical, emotional as well as psychological. The hostility of some feminists to pornography and sado-masochistic activities relies on the argument that representations of violence can cause violence, and that sexual behaviour which flirts with power imbalances can sustain existing power relations.

The most powerful argument against this, also advanced by feminists, though of a rather different persuasion, is that attempts to suppress potentially harmful representations or fantasies do not in practice eliminate them but on the contrary reinforce their transgressive power. Jessica Benjamin has argued that our culture is facing a crisis of what she describes as 'male rationality', and a resurgence of erotic fantasy. She goes on:

A politics that denies these issues, that tries to sanitize or

> rationalizes the erotic, fantastic components of human life, will
> not defeat domination, but only vacate the field. [14]

This, she believes, means the avoidance both of a simple libertarian acceptance and of moral condemnation. The primary task is to understand. And what should the basis of our understanding be? Surely it must be a recognition that the complex forces that shape our sexualities — biological, potentialities, unconscious motivations and desires, and social organization — produce many needs and wishes which often go beyond our dispassionate understanding or the canons of political correctness. Sexual excitement, Lynne Segal writes, 'is generated by, and in the service of, a multitude of needs, not all of them "nice"' [15]. This implies, rightly in my opinion, that sexuality is too difficult and elusive an idea to be tied away into neat compartments of right or wrong. We need to be alive to its ambivalent and ambiguous qualities, and act accordingly.

Sexual 'choice', then, suggests a recognition of limits as well as possibilities, hazardous paths as much as positive goals. It must also, however, take into account another reality: the fact of conflicting choices, opposed goals. As I have already noted the debate on abortion has produced ultimately irreconcilable 'rights': those of the 'unborn child' against those of the mother who claims a right to control her own fertility. Here there are massively different conceptions in conflict: different views of what constitutes 'life', and opposing claims over the absolute autonomy of the body. But even within the broad parameters of a common social and political affiliation the 'right to choose' can have different meanings in different contexts. The feminist claim to a right to choose abortion must also involve a right to choose *not* to have an abortion. In a society where black women or poor women may be encouraged (either for racist and/or population policy reasons) to limit their family size, a call for the right to abortion will appear narrowly exclusive. In Britain in the mid-1980s this has led to a shift amongst feminists away from a campaign simply for abortion rights to a wider campaign to ensure 'reproductive rights' for women as a whole — to embrace campaigns against compulsory sterilization or compulsory abortion as well as for the rights of women to terminate their pregnancies, if they choose.

The context in which choice is demanded and operative is, therefore, critical. Sexual values cannot be detached from the wider social values we hold, and these themselves are increasingly diverse. We saw earlier that the world of sexuality is fragmented by a number of other relations: of race, gender and class particularly. This means that different groups will endorse different perspectives and develop often strikingly opposed priorities. The white feminist critique of the family, for example, will appear ethnocentric and oppressive to black feminists struggling to defend their families against racist immigration procedures which may work to split families. Similarly, the priority given by gay and lesbian movements to 'coming out', to openly declaring your sexual preferences as a means of affirming their validity, often conflicts with the need felt by black lesbians and gay men in a racist culture to affirm their political identity with their communities of origin, whatever the family and sexual orthodoxies prevailing there [16]. A discourse of choice must therefore be based not only on a recognition of different individual needs and goals, but of different means of living them.

There is another important factor that needs to be stressed. The priority given to diversity and choice runs the danger of appearing as a purely individual activity, with each isolated monad having to make his or her choice in the face of a multitude of options. The lessons of the past twenty years of sexual politics suggests, however, that it is collective activity that ultimately provides the real guarantee of individual choice. The emergence of new political subjects — feminists, lesbian and gays, and other sexual minorities alongside blacks, peace campaigners, ecologists and others — has dramatised the change that is taking place in the political ecology of the West, with often profound affects on the workings of its representative systems. But more crucially for this discussion, they have demonstratively made possible the new individual self-assertion of women, homosexuals and others that has changed the sexual scene of the West. The new vocabulary of sexual needs and desires is overwhelmingly a product of what can best be called 'collective self activity'.

This is the point where sexual politics inevitably returns to its wider social context, and its moral and political alignments. The choices we are confronted with are decided in the end not by anything intrinsic to sexuality itself but by the wider set of values and goals which we embrace. This brings us back to the ideal of democracy. A sexual democracy necessarily implies a wider process of democratization in which the barriers that restrict individual potentiality and growth — the barriers of economic exploitations and class divisions, racial oppressions and gender inequalities, moral authoritarianism and educational disadvantage, poverty and insecurity — are progressively dismantled. This must not be taken to imply that real difficulties, real divisions of need and interest, real conflicts of priority or of desire, will, or ought to, disappear. The aim, on the contrary, ought to be to maximize the means by which these differences and conflicts can be resolved democratically.

As society becomes ever more complex it is likely that the patterns of individual sexual needs and relationships will be in ever more exotic flux. I have suggested in this essay that we should be more ready than we have been to go with the flood: to fully accept the possibilities opened up by a growing social and moral pluralism, to embrace, in all their accompanying ambiguities and potential conflicts, the merits of sexual diversity and choice. The sexual tradition offered a fundamentally monolithic construct which we know as 'sexuality'. In recent years its pretensions have been punctured, its dubious origins revealed and its restrictive effects exposed. We have deconstructed the idea of sexuality. It is now perhaps time to start thinking afresh about individual needs and aspirations, and the social policies that can satisfy them; to think about the proper balance between private pleasures and public policies. A genuine acceptance of moral pluralism seems the only appropriate starting point.

REFERENCES

[1] Michael Ignatieff, *The Needs of Strangers,* Chatto & Windus, London (1984), p. 135.
[2] Gayle Rubin, 'Thinking sex', in Carole S. Vance (ed.), *Pleasure and Danger. Exploring Female Sexuality,* Routledge & Kegan Paul, Boston and London (1984), p. 285.
[3] Magnus Hirschfeld, 'Presidential address: The development and scope of sexology', in Norman Haire (ed.), *World League for Sexual Reform: Proceedings of the Third Congress,* London (1930), p. xiv.
[4] Compare Bernard Williams, *Ethics and the Limits of Philosophy,* Fontana Press/Collins, London (1985), p. 1.
[5] Michel Foucault, *The History of Sexuality,* Vol. 1, *An Introduction,* trans. Robert Hurley, Allen Lane, London (1979), p. 149.
[6] Michel Foucault, 'On the genealogy of ethics: an overview of work in progress', in Paul Rabinow (ed.), *The Foucault Reader,* Pantheon Books, New York (1984), p. 343.
[7] Michel Foucault, *Histoire de la sexualite:* 2, *L'Usage des plaisirs;* 3, *Le Souci de soi,* Editions Gallimard, Paris (1984).
[8] Michel Foucault, 'Sexual choice, sexual acts', *Salmagundi* Nos. 58–59, Fall 1982, Winter 1983, p. 12.
[9] Rubin, op. cit., p. 278.
[10] Alvin Gouldner, *For Sociology,* Allen Lane, London (1973), p. 295.
[11] Rosalind Coward, *Female Desire. Women's Sexuality Today,* Paladin, London (1984), p. 78.
[12] Rubin, op. cit., p. 288.
[13] Havelock Ellis, *The Psychology of Sex,* William Heinemann, London (1946; first published 1933), p. 184.

[14] Jessica Benjamin, 'Master and slave. The fantasy of erotic domination', in Ann Snitow, Christine Stansell and Sharon Thompson (eds.), *Desire: The Politics of Sexuality,* Virago, London (1984), p. 308.

[15] Lynne Segal, 'Sensual uncertainty, or why the clitoris is not enough', in Sue Cartledge and Joanna Ryan (eds.), *Sex and Love. New Thoughts on Old Contradictions,* The Women's Press, London (1983), p. 45.

[16] See Valerie Amos and Pratibha Parmar, 'Challenging imperial feminism', *Feminist Review,* **17**, Autumn 1984; Barbara Ormolade, 'Hearts of darkness', in 'Snitow *et al.,* op cit.

Suggestions for further reading

The perspective outlined in this essay is elaborated in greater detail in the three books I have written on the social organization of sex: Jeffrey Weeks, *Coming Out. Homosexual Politics in Britain from the 19th Century to the Present*, Quartet, London (1977); *Sex, Politics and Society. The Regulation of Sexuality since 1800*, Longman, Harlow (1981); *Sexuality and its Discontents. Meanings, Myths and Modern Sexualities*, Routledge & Kegan Paul, London (1985). These contain detailed notes and references which may be pursued for further reading.

No contemporary writer on sexuality can escape the influence of Michel Foucault, even if the end result is a total rejection of his works. His views are polemically summed up in *The History of Sexuality, Volume 1, An Introduction*, Allen Lane, London (1979). At the time of writing, the next two volumes of *The History*, published just before his death, had not been translated from the French. They are different in style and in content from Volume 1, but they are fascinating nonetheless: *Histoire de la sexualité; 2, L'Usage des plaisirs*, and 3, *Le Souci de soi*, Editions Gallimard, Paris (1984). His interviews often provide many clarifying insights concerning his overall project. See especially *Power/Knowledge: Selected Interviews and Other Writings 1972–1977*, edited by Colin Gordon, Harvester Press, Brighton (1980), and *The Foucault Reader*, edited by Paul Rabinow, Pantheon Books, New York (1984). Although no substitute for reading the originals, there is a growing corpus of commentaries on Foucault but as yet, surprisingly, none specifically on his writings on sexuality. For a useful guide to his work see Barry Smart, *Michel Foucault*, Ellis Horwood/ Tavistock, Chichester and London (1985).

Recent sociological debates on sex can be pursued in: J. H. Gagnon and William Simon, *Sexual Conduct. The Social Sources of Human Sexuality*, Hutchinson, London (1973); John H. Gagnon, *Human Sexualities*, Scott, Foresman and Co., Glenview, Illinois (1977); Kenneth Plummer, *Sexual Stigma. An Interactionist Account*, Routledge & Kegan Paul, London

(1975); Mike Brake (ed.), *Human Sexual Relations. A Reader,* Penguin, Harmondsworth (1982). For psychoanalysis, the starting point should be Sigmund Freud, *Three Essays on the Theory of Sexuality,* first published in 1905 and much revised over the next 20 years. It is available in Volume 7 of *The Standard Edition of the Complete Psychological Works of Sigmund Freud* edited by James Strachey, Hogarth Press and the Institute of Psychoanalysis, London (1953). In Britain it is available in paperback in Volume 7 of The Pelican Freud Library, *On Sexuality,* Penguin, Harmondsworth (1977), together with other useful papers. Discussions of the significance of Freud to contemporary analyses of sexuality can be found in: Juliet Mitchell, *Psychoanalysis and Feminism,* Allen Lane, London (1973); Rosalind Coward, *Patriarchal Precedents. Sexuality and Social Relations,* Routledge & Kegan Paul, London (1983); *Female Desire. Women's Sexuality Today,* Paladin, London (1984); and Jacques Lacan and the Ecole Freudienne, *Feminine Sexuality,* edited by Juliet Mitchell and Jacqueline Rose, Macmillan, London (1982). The two books by Coward are also highly relevant to current debates about the nature of sexuality.

Two collections of articles contain a wide range of material on the theory, history, sociology, poetry and politics (especially feminist politics) of sex: Ann Snitow, Christine Stansell, and Sharon Thompson (eds.), *Desire. The Politics of Sexuality,* Virago, London (1983), published in the USA as: *Powers of Desire: The Politics of Sexuality,* Monthly Review Press, New York (1983); and Carole S. Vance (ed.), *Pleasure and Danger. Exploring Female Sexuality,* Routledge & Kegan Paul, London, Boston (1984). A long essay in the latter by Gayle Rubin, 'Thinking sex: notes for a radical theory of the politics of sexuality' is particularly important. Both these volumes contain useful articles about the interconnections between race and sexuality. For further discussions of sex, gender and race see *Feminist Review,* **17**, 1984.

A helpful, if variable, survey of Western attitudes to sex can be found in: Philippe Ariès and André Bejin (eds.), *Western Sexuality, Practice and Precept in Past and Present Times,* Basil Blackwell, Oxford (1985). Lawrence Stone's massive, *The Family, Sex and Marriage in England 1500–1800,* Weidenfeld & Nicolson, London (1977), provides an overview of (chiefly upper class) attitudes for the period. A growing and very important literature on the history of homosexuality provides new insights into the 'invention of sexuality'. For major interventions see: John Boswell, *Social Tolerance and Homosexuality. Gay People in Western Europe from the Beginning of the Christian Era to the Fourteenth Century,* University of Chicago Press, Chicago and London (1980); Alan Bray, *Homosexuality in Renaissance England,* Gay Men's Press, London (1982); Jonathan Ned Katz, *Gay/Lesbian Almanac,* Harper & Row, New York (1983); Lillian

Faderman, *Surpassing the Love of Men. Romantic Friendship and Love between Women from the Renaissance to the Present,* Junction Books, London (1980); Kenneth Plummer (ed), *The Making of the Modern Homosexual,* Hutchinson, London (1981); and Estelle B. Freedman *et al., The Lesbian Issue. Essays from Signs,* University of Chicago Press, Chicago and London (1985).

On the biology and psychology of sexual differences see John Archer and Barbara Lloyd, *Sex and Gender,* Penguin, Harmondsworth (1982); John Nicholson, *Men and Women. How Different are They,* Oxford University Press, Oxford and New York (1984); Ann Oakley, *Sex, Gender and Society,* revised edition, Gower, Aldershot (1985); Steven Rose, Leon J. Kamin and R. C. Lewontin, *Not in our Genes. Biology, Ideology and Human Nature,* Penguin Harmondsworth (1984); Julian Henriques *et al., Changing the Subject. Psychology, Social Regulation and Subjectivity,* Methuen London and New York (1984); Andy Metcalf and Martin Humphries, *The Sexuality of Men,* Pluto, London (1985); Angela Mc-Robbie and Mica Nava, *Gender and Generation,* Macmillan, London (1984); and Janet Sayers, *Sexual Contradictions,* Tavistock, London (1986).

Recent discussions of the meaning of 'sexual perversion' can be found in Robert J Stoller, *Perversion. The Erotic Form of Hatred,* Quartet, London (1977); Janine Chasseguet-Smirgel, *Creativity and Perversion,* Free Association Books, London (1985); and the essays in K. Howells (ed.), *Sexual Diversity,* Blackwell, Oxford (1984).

Contemporary political controversies about sex can be followed in: Barbara Ehrenreich, *The Hearts of Men. American Dreams and the Flight from Commitment,* Pluto, London (1983), first published by Anchor Press/ Doubleday, New York (1983); Elizabeth Wilson, *What is to be Done about Violence against Women?,* Penguin, Harmondsworth (1983); Dennis Altman, *The Homosexualization of America, the Americanization of the Homosexual,* St. Martin's Press, New York (1982); *AIDS and the Mind of America,* New York, Doubleday (1986), published in Britain as *AIDS and the New Puritans, ,* Pluto, London (1986); Sue Cartledge and Joanna Ryan (eds.), *Sex and Love. New Thoughts on Old Contradictions,* The Women's Press, London (1983).

Index